Compact
Guide

PUBLISHER

Metropolis International
222 Kensal Road
London W10 5BN
England

Telephone:
+44-(0)20-8964-4242

Fax:
+44-(0)20-8964-4141

E-mail:
admin@for-less.com

Web site:
http://www.for-less.com

ABBREVIATIONS

☎ Telephone Number
🕒 Opening times

Publisher Information

First published in Great Britain in 1999 by Metropolis International (UK) Ltd.

ISBN 1 901811 50 6

COPYRIGHT

Copyright © Metropolis International (UK) Limited, 1999.

for less, for less logos and *for less guidebooks* are trademarks of Metropolis International (UK) Limited.

All rights reserved. No part of this book may be reproduced or utilized in any form or by any means, electronic or mechanical, including photocopying, recording or by any information storage retrieval system, without permission in writing from the publishers.

DISCLAIMER

Assessments of attractions, hotels, museums and so forth are based on the author's impressions and therefore contain an element of subjective opinion that may not reflect the opinion of the publishers.

The contents of this publication are believed to be correct at the time of printing. However, details such as opening times will change over time. We would advise you to call ahead to confirm important information.

All organizations offering discounts in this guidebook have a contract with the publisher to give genuine discounts to holders of valid *for less* vouchers.

The publisher and/or its agents will not be responsible if any establishment breaches its contract (although it will attempt to secure compliance) or if any establishment changes ownership and the new owners refuse to honour the contract.

Care has been taken to ensure that discounts are only offered at reputable establishments, however, the publisher and/or its agents cannot accept responsibility for the quality of merchandise or service provided, nor for errors or inaccuracies in this guidebook.

The publisher will not be held responsible for any loss, damage, injury, expense or inconvenience sustained by any person, howsoever caused, as a result of information or advice contained in this guide except in so far as the law prevents the exclusion of such liability.

Contents

Introduction to Florence	**4-7**
History of Florence	**8-9**
Exploring Florence	**10-51**
Central Florence	10-30
Northern Florence	31-39
The Arno and Southern Florence	40-51
Beyond the City	**52-55**
Dining	**56-57**
Shopping	**58-59**
Nightlife	**60-61**
Visitor Information	**62-67**
Index	**68**
Vouchers	**69-71**
Customer Response Card	**71-72**

HOW TO OBTAIN DISCOUNTS

Many of the museums and attractions in this guide offer discounts to holders of this book.

Museums and attractions which offer a discount are highlighted in pink in the text and designated by the following symbol in the margins:

To obtain your discount, simply hand in the appropriate voucher from the back of the book when you purchase your ticket.

Introduction to Florence

View of Florence from the Forte di Belvedere

The skyline of Florence is one of the great products of unintentional town planning. The vast bulk of the cathedral dome, towering over the low red roofs of the city, makes an unforgettable sight.

The best way to see the city is on foot. The centre is small and many of the streets are pedestrianised, with intriguing alleys and narrow thoroughfares branching off from imposing squares.

Florence is a city to enjoy indoors, too, for it offers a rich and varied selection of galleries, museums and palaces. As the centre of the artistic movement, known as the Renaissance, which bridged the gap between the Middle Ages and the modern world, the city not surprisingly has some of the world's finest works of art – many of which are still in the palace, church or monastery for which they were originally intended.

The Renaissance germinated in Florence in the 1290s under Dante and Giotto, who influenced succeeding writers and artists. The movement was based on the rediscovery – and the close scrutiny – of ancient Greek and Roman literature, art and architecture.

Using classical forms, artists developed a new language of rationalisation, scientific experimentation and understanding. Gradually the notion of freedom of

Did You Know...?

Florence has around 380,000 inhabitants and is visited by over 3 million people every year.

Introduction to Florence · 5

individual expression gained hold, leading to the artistic revolution of the 15th century.

Brunelleschi was the first to put the new theories into architectural practice, with his magnificent cathedral dome of the 1420s. Masaccio and Uccello pioneered perspective in painting, Donatello and Michelangelo explored sculpture and Filippo Lippi and Fra' Angelico spent years creating elaborate frescoes in their monasteries.

The transition between the stylised forms of the Middle Ages and the highly individual expression of the Renaissance is best seen in the frescoes in the **Capella Branacci**, as well as Masaccio's Holy Trinity and Uccello's striking frescoes in **Santa Maria Novella**.

The two heavyweight collections that are top of any visitor's list are the fabulous paintings of the **Uffizi** and the sculptures in the **Bargello**, both staggering collections from one of the richest artistic periods in history. Both museums are small enough to be manageable in a single visit, yet interesting enough to enable visitors to spend many hours examining the exquisite detail and craftsmanship of individual pieces.

Art is not confined to the many galleries in Florence, however, but is spread evenly throughout the city's great religious foundations.

Don't Miss

The **Bóboli Gardens** (page 44), the only green area in the centre of the city.

Florence is a city of unrivalled artistic beauty

6 · Introduction to Florence

The River Arno

Santa Maria Novella has frescoes by Uccello and **Santa Croce** houses a series by Giotto, alongside the tombs of Michelangelo and Machiavelli. The frescoes by Fra' Angelico are the main attraction of **Santa Maria del Carmine**, and **San Lorenzo** is famed for the powerful sculpture in Michelangelo's **Medici Chapel**.

On top of such a list of staggering jewels, the city's main religious complex is one of the most memorable to be seen. The vast marble bulk of the **Duomo**, the octagonal **Baptistery** with its famous carved bronze doors, and Giotto's monumental **Campanile** together form the focal point of the city, to which visitors return again and again. The **Museo dell'Opera del Duomo** tells the story of the building and restoring of this great trio of buildings, as well as the masterpieces they contain.

Don't Miss

Florence has its own tradition of celebrating New Year in March, when a big fair is held in Piazza Santissima Anunnziata.

The Medici, as rulers of the city for three centuries, are largely responsible for Florence's rise as an artistic centre. Under their patronage, a string of famous architects, artists, sculptors and thinkers worked here. These figures included Brunelleschi, Donatello, Galileo, Bronzino, Ghirlandaio, Botticelli, Michelangelo, Leonardo da Vinci, Masaccio, Macchiavelli, Raphael and Uccello.

Visitors can gain an invaluable insight into the world of the fabulously wealthy Medici in the **Palazzo Vecchio**, **Palazzo Pitti** and **Palazzo Medici-Ruccardu**, as well as in the ordered vistas of the **Giardino di Bóboli** (Bóboli Gardens) and the sombre mausoleums of **San Lorenzo**.

Introduction to Florence · 7

Florence is also an active working city, with thriving banking, industrial and manufacturing centres. Its leatherware, handmade paper and stylish fashions are admired throughout the world. Even for those without the money or inclination to buy, it is easy to spend a few pleasant hours wandering the streets and window-shopping in the pristine boutiques. Alternatively, settle in a café and take some time to admire the constant parade of immaculately turned-out locals going about their business.

As a vibrant university town that attracts students of fine art from around the globe, there is also a young and lively nightlife to be discovered.

The city is at the core of a part of Italy that takes its food very seriously indeed. Tuscany has produced some of the most influential dishes of Italian cuisine, including its finest homemade ice-creams.

If you have sufficient time, Florence is also an ideal starting point from which to make a number of fascinating day trips. The glorious rolling Tuscan countryside to the south of the city is the **Chianti** area, whose wine-producing tradition is recognised all over the world. Also easily reached from Florence are the beautiful medieval walled town of **Siena**, the soaring towers of **San Gimignano**, the Etruscan legacy of **Volterra** and, of course, the architectural highlights of **Pisa**, which include the celebrated **Leaning Tower**.

IF YOU DO ONE THING . . .

1. If you visit one museum . . . the **Museo Bargello** (page 26)

2. If you visit one church . . . **Santa Croce** (page 27)

3. If you cross one bridge . . . **Ponte Vecchio** (page 40)

4. If you go to one theatre . . . **Teatro Verdi** (page 61)

5. If you walk in one park . . . **Giardino di Bóboli** (page 44)

6. If you dine in one restaurant . . **Caffè Gilli** (page 57)

7. If you go to one art gallery . . . the **Uffizi** (page 23)

8. If you go to one market . . . **Mercato Centrale** (page 58)

9. If you go on one excursion . . . **Siena** (page 54)

10. If you stroll in one square . . . **Piazza della Signoria** (page 21)

History of Florence

Florence's origins date back to 59 BC, when **Julius Caesar** founded Florentia, the 'city of flowers'. The site was chosen due to a narrow crossing in the river, and a bridge was soon constructed, on the site of today's Ponte Vecchio. Florentia quickly grew as the river brought trading vessels, and by AD 1000 it had become an important religious centre. In 1115 it was recognised as the area's most important settlement, and was granted the status of a commune, or independent city.

The textile industry enabled the city to grow rapidly. Art and craft guilds were established and soon flourished, alongside the increasingly wealthy religious orders that built the elaborate convents and churches. The following century saw decline, with a devastating fire in 1333 and the Black Death in 1348, which wiped out half the city's population. But it was also this century that saw the blossoming of Florence's artistic life, with the talents of Dante and Giotto dictating the pace.

The **Medici** dynasty, who ruled Florence from 1434 to 1737, were perhaps the greatest artistic patrons the world has ever seen. This wealth attracted the finest artists to the city and accelerated the development of new techniques of expression, culminating in the rich blossoming of the arts now known as the Renaissance. The movement stressed harmony of design through mathematical principles and signified man's increasing confidence in his own abilities. Even the inspirational sermons of the nomadic monk Savonarola on the subject of decadence in 1490s' society did not convince a population becoming used to luxury, and he was quickly disposed of.

Florence became a Grand Duchy in 1570 under **Cosimo I**, Grand Duke of Tuscany, who was responsible for building the Uffizi, the world's first government office complex, and extending the Palazzo Vecchio. But not all Medici rulers were benevolent in their outlook, and economic decline, political machinations and war led to the dynasty's downfall.

Reflections

'Italian in the mouth of Italians is a deep-voiced stream, with unexpected cataracts and boulders to preserve it from monotony' – E.M. Forster

History of Florence · 9

In 1737 Florence passed to the **House of Lorraine**, part of the Austrian **Habsburg** family, who ruled until the French invaded in 1799 and Napoleon's cousin Elisa Baciocchi was made Tuscany's **Grand Duchess**.

Florence was declared capital of the unified Kingdom of Italy in 1861. Town planner **Giuseppi Poggi** began his destructive campaign to turn Florence into a grand capital, by flattening the Renaissance city and creating monumental squares and public buildings. The 14th-century city walls were torn down and a number of buildings demolished before an international outcry prevented more damage, and in 1871 Rome was made the capital.

During the Second World War, Florence was spared – apart from the bridges that were all systematically blown up by the Nazis, with the exception of the Ponte Vecchio. Michelangelo's Ponte Triníta was picked piece by piece from the river and reassembled to original plans. The most severe damage Florence has experienced in recent times was caused by the flood in 1966. The waters of the River Arno rose 6 metres (19 feet) above street level, destroying many works of art. Restoration still continues on some damaged pieces.

Statue of David in the Piazza della Signorina

Florence's economy now depends largely on tourism. Young gentlemen on their Grand Tour during the 18th century first discovered the joys of the city, and the building of better roads and a railway in the 19th century attracted people in their thousands. Today, Florence's popularity as a cultural tourist destination is greater than ever.

Exploring Florence: Central Florence

Central Florence

Santa Maria del Fiore, the Duomo

The focus of the Florentine skyline is the vast bulk of Brunelleschi's eight-sided dome on the cathedral Santa Maria del Fiore, popularly known as the **Duomo**. The splendid dome towers above the city's terracotta rooftops, drawing attention to the architectural masterpiece that is widely considered to be the first Renaissance building.

In 1294, sculptor Arnolfo di Cambio was chosen to design the largest church in the Roman Catholic world, to reflect a proud city at its cultural peak. The 153-metre (500-foot) nave has the capacity to hold up to 30,000 people.

Cambio was in his grave when the problem of building the largest dome ever attempted arose. Sculptor Filippo Brunelleschi arrogantly declared he could build across the 42-metre (140-foot) span without using scaffolding. He began work in 1420, building rings of bricks that supported both themselves and the next ring. Within just 16 years the entire 106-metre (347-foot) high dome was finished.

In contrast to the warm red-orange dome, the green, pink and white marble facing of the exterior appears cold and hard, but fittingly intricate. The oldest section is the south side, while the main facade dates from just 1887 and is built in the style of Giotto.

Duomo

Piazza del Duomo
☎ 055 230-2885
🕒 Mon-Fri: 8.30am-6.20pm. Sat: 8.30am-5pm. Sun: closed.

Exploring Florence: Central Florence · 11

The dimly lit interior is a huge, austere space. The marble floor features a labyrinth motif from the 1550s, while the garish fresco beneath the dome is of the *Last Judgement*, undertaken by Vasari and Zuccari in the 1570s.

On entering, there is a bust of Brunelleschi in the right-hand bay. Also noteworthy are the two *trompe l'oeil* frescoes on the left wall, one of English military leader John Harwood by Paolo Uccello, the other of Niccolò da Tolentino by Andrea del Castagno. In the next bay is the famous panel of *Dante Explaining the Divine Comedy* by Domenico do Michelino. At the far end of the church, beneath the altar, is the tomb by Ghiberti containing the relics of St. Zanobi.

Battistero

Piazza San Giovanni
☎ 055 230-2885
🕓 Mon-Sat: 12noon-6.30pm. Sun: 8.30am-1.30pm.
Admission charge.

If you have a head for heights, you can ascend the dome by means of a narrow staircase. The views over the city from the top are staggering. Otherwise, head for the crypt to explore the substantial remains of the original 5th-century church of Santa Reparata and the tomb of Brunelleschi.

The **Battistero** (Baptistery) **di San Giovanni** was completed in 1150, a copy of an earlier design that had stood here since the 7th century. Situated directly in front of the Duomo's main entrance, this octagonal cathedral annex boasts green and white marble motifs, as well as its famous gilded bronze doors.

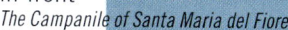
The Campanile of Santa Maria del Fiore

Illustrating both books of the Bible, these three sets of doors formed one of the wonders of the medieval world. The oldest are Andrea Pisano's south doors of 1330, whose 28 panels depict in detail significant scenes from the life of St. John the Baptist, the city's patron saint.

12 · Exploring Florence: Central Florence

Campanile

Piazza del Duomo
☎ 055 230-2885
🕐 Mon-Sun: 9am-6pm.
Admission charge.

Museo del Bigallo

Piazza San Giovanni 6
☎ 055 230-2885
🕐 Mon-Sat: 8.15am-
1.30pm. Sun: closed.

Museo dell'Opera del Duomo

Piazza del Duomo 9
☎ 055 230-2885
🕐 Apr-Oct: Mon-Sat:
9am-6.50pm. Nov-Mar:
Mon-Sat: 9am-6.20pm.
Sun: 9am-1.20pm.
Admission charge.

The Black Death halted progress on the building until 1400, when Lorenzo Ghiberti – at just 24 years old – beat both Donatello and Brunelleschi in a competition for the commission. His north door has life-like scenes from the New Testament, and the east door depicts Old Testament scenes alongside a number of portraits of famous artists.

The interior features include a lining of black and white marble, a floor bearing mosaics illustrating the signs of the zodiac, and columns reminiscent of Rome's Pantheon. Above the huge font, which dates from 1371, is a fabulous 13th-century ceiling mosaic, which depicts, among other things, the *Last Judgement*.

Designed in 1334 by Giotto, the **Campanile**, or belltower, is a sheer cliff of marble that rises to 84 metres (276 feet), just 6 metres (20 feet) shorter than the dome. Before his death in 1337, Giotto had completed the first storey of the tower with hexagonal bas-reliefs depicting the *Creation and Fall of Man*.

The work was taken over by Andrea Pisano, who built the next two stages in a similar style, with illustrations of the planet, virtues, sacraments and liberal arts. The top three floors were completed by Francesco Talenti, who lightened the structure with an airy open mullion window on each facade. Niches contain statues of kings, prophets, patriarchs and sybils. Inside, a staircase of 414 steps leads to the terrace and its wonderful view from the top.

The **Museo del Bigallo** is accessed via the Gothic frontage of the Loggia del Bigallo, which was built in 1358 for the Misericordia, a charitable mission who cared for the sick after the plague.

It is a tiny museum of religious art. Most of the pieces date from between 1250 and 1400. The most notable exhibit is a fresco of the *Madonna della Misericordia* of 1342, showing the earliest known view of the city – interestingly, without the cathedral.

Behind the Duomo, the **Museo dell'Opera**

Exploring Florence: Central Florence · 13

del Duomo (Cathedral Works Museum) oversees the conservation of the city's three main religious buildings. It is crammed with items that were taken from the exterior of the cathedral, baptistery and belltower and to protect them against weather and pollution erosion.

The exhibition begins with archaeological finds from the site's older church of Santa Reparta. A room devoted to the construction of the Duomo we see today features several models used during its construction, as well as projected Brunelleschi facades that came to nothing. There are also 15th-century masons' tools, pulleys and winches.

Of most interest are pieces from the buildings themselves: a haunting *Madonna* by Arnolfo from the original facade; a *Pietà* by Michelangelo, intended for his own tomb, but unfinished; Donatello's wooden *Madonna* and reliefs for the Campanile; and Ghiberti's revered east door from the baptistery.

The so-called **Palazzo Nonfinito**, or 'Unfinished Palace', was begun in 1593 and was still awaiting completion when the **Museo Nazionale di Antropologia ed Ethnologia** (Anthropology and Ethnology Museum) took up residence here in 1869. This folk museum incorporates items relating to culture, costume and tradition from all over the world.

The ground floor houses the Indian collection. Upstairs, twelve rooms are filled with African artefacts, including wooden sculptures and Abyssinian finds. Four rooms devoted to the Americas include some well-preserved

Palazzo Nonfinito

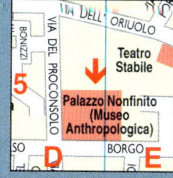

Proconsolo 12
☎ 055 239-6449
🕒 Wed-Mon: 9.30am-1pm. Tue: closed.

The Baptistery

14 · Exploring Florence: Central Florence

Peruvian mummies. The Asian department has some fine Polynesian carvings, as well as a range of curiosities collected in 1779 by Captain Cook on his extensive travels around the Pacific Islands, including human heads.

Probably the best-known church in Florence, **Santa Maria Novella** was started by monks of the austere Dominican order in 1246. However, it was only finished when Alberti added the famous scrolls on the main facade in 1470 to hide the roofline. Blending Renaissance principles with the Romanesque lower facade, the volutes were widely copied and formed an important element of Baroque style.

Santa Maria Novella

Inside, the nave is characterised by Gothic pillars that are positioned gradually closer towards the altar, which creates the illusion of length. On the left side of the nave, Masaccio's *Trinity* was the first work of the late Gothic period to use perspective – and as such must have stunned its first viewers. In the chancel, known as the Tornabuoni Chapel, are Ghirlandaio's famous frescoes of the lives of St. John and the Virgin Mary, which contain vivid portraits of artists and philosophers of the day.

Next door, the Cappella Gondi contains Brunelleschi's only work in wood – a crucifix. To the left is the Strozzi Chapel, whose frescoes by Nardo di Cione were inspired by Dante's *Divine Comedy*. On the

Exploring Florence: Central Florence · 15

right side of the chancel is the Filippo Strozzi Chapel, with Filippino Lippi's frescoes of St. John, used by Boccaccio as inspiration for *The Decameron*. The altarpiece itself was carved by Nardo's brother Orcagna.

The **Museo e Chiostri Monumentali,** housed in the cloisters and several adjoining rooms, is entered from the north side of the nave. It contains valuable examples of Florentine painting from the 14th and 15th centuries. The Romanesque **Green Cloister** displays some exemplary marvels of the Renaissance. These include Paolo Uccello's *Noah and the Flood* frescoes. This depiction of dozens of biblical characters and scenes was painted in 1425, but seriously damaged in the 1966 flood. The former chapter hall or **Spanish Chapel** contains cautionary frescoes on the themes of salvation and damnation. These were created by Andrea di Bonaiuto and his students in the 1360s.

The museum is also home to a collection of textiles, sculptures, embroidery and jewellery from the treasury of Santa Maria Novella. The highlights include the 16th-century vestments of St. Thomas and the Reliquary of the Title of the Cross, which dates from the end of the 14th century or earlier.

The Museo e Chiostri Monumentali and many of the other museums in this guide are part of the **Comune di Firenze Museo Fiorentini**. With a **Museo Fiorentini** carnet, which can be purchased at any of the participating museums and galleries, you can visit all ten of them at a discount of 50% on each admission price. Holders of this guide are entitled to 2 carnets for the price of 1 with the voucher on page 71. See the individual entries throughout the guide for details of the other participating museums and art galleries.

To the right of Santa Maria Novella is a cemetery, whose walls carry the badges of wealthy citizens.

The **Museo Alinari** holds permanent photographic exhibitions which document Florence in the 19th century. The three

Santa Maria Novella

Piazza di Santa Maria Novella
☎ 055 210-113
⏰ Mon-Fri: 7am-12noon & 3pm-6pm. Sat: 7am-12.15pm & 3pm-5pm. Sun: 7am-12noon & 3pm-6pm.

Museo e Chiostri Monumentali

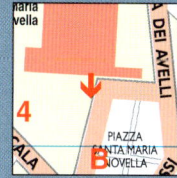

Piazza di Santa Maria Novella
☎ 055 210-113
⏰ Mon-Thu & Sat: 9am-2pm. Sun: 8am-1pm. Fri: closed.
Admission charge.
Musei Fiorentini discount – 2 carnets for the price of 1 (carnet comprises 10 coupons for 50% discount on admission to participating museums and galleries) with voucher on page 71.

16 · Exploring Florence: Central Florence

Ognissanti

Borgo Ognissanti 42
☎ 055 239-8700
⏱ Mon-Sun: 8am-12noon and 4pm-7pm.

Museo Alinari

Piazza di Santa Maria Novella
☎ 055 239-5239
⏱ This museum will reopen in Spring 1999.

Museo Marino Marini (for less)

Piazza San Pancrazio
☎ 055 219-432
⏱ Mon & Wed-Sat: 10am-5pm. Sun: 10am-1pm. Tue & Sun: closed. Admission charge.
Musei Fiorentini discount – 2 carnets for the price of 1 (carnet comprises 10 coupons for 50% discount on admission to participating museums and galleries) with voucher on page 71.

Alinari brothers started taking photographs in the 1840s, producing high-quality postcards, art books and souvenirs for the wealthy people passing through Florence on their Grand Tour.

The **Palazzo Rucellai**, which houses the photographic archives, was built in the 15th century by Rossellino, to a design by Alberti. It is the first nobleman's house in Florence to follow classical rules. The distinctive facade has three superimposed orders of pillars, paying homage to the Colosseum in Rome.

The building contains a chapel where Giovanni Rucellai is buried, his tomb modelled on the Holy Sepulchre, Christ's tomb in Jerusalem.

To the west lies the church of **Ognissanti** (All Saints), which was founded in 1251 by the Umiliati order from Lombardy, whose cloth weaving industry was largely responsible for turning Florence into one of the most powerful cities in the country.

The nave was lavishly painted with frescoes during the 15th century. Ghirlandaio's *Madonna della Misericordia* (1472) and *St. Jerome* (1480) share wall space with Botticelli's *St. Augustine* of 1480. The refectory has Ghirlandaio's fresco of *The Last Supper*, which also dates from 1480.

When the Franciscans took over the buildings in the 1630s, they redesigned the church into one of the earliest Baroque buildings in Florence, although the original campanile was retained.

An interesting historical note is that this was the parish church of the Vespucci family, one of whom, Amerigo, gave his name to the New World. His grave can be seen here.

Housed in the former convent of **San Pancrazio**, the intimate collection of the **Museo Marino Marini** is devoted to the works of Marini, a sculptor born in Pistoia in 1901 who died in 1980.

Marini studied art in Florence and went on to become famous throughout Italy for his raw, emotional bronze sculptures and paintings. The collection features 200

Exploring Florence: Central Florence · 17

works, many on the theme of horses and their riders. The best of these include the wooden figure of a *Swimmer* and a painting called *Gentleman on Horseback*, both from the 1930s.

The collection, which also comprises plaster models, paintings and drawings, provides a good representation of Marini's command of a variety of techniques and his interest in the expressive possibilities of form. It is an important acquisition of contemporary art for the city.

Palazzo Strozzi

The huge golden Baroque **Palazzo Corsini** on the riverfront was built in the 1640s by the wealthy, art-collecting Corsini nobles.

The lavish interiors play host to Florence's leading private art collection – the Galleria Corsini on the second floor. The Italian and European works of the 16th and 17th century include pieces by Bellini and Pontormo, allegorical figures by Filippino Lippi and Raphael's portrait of Julius II.

Palazzo Corsini

Lungarno Corsini
☎ 055 218-994
🕐 Call for appointment.

The austere 11th-century monastic church of **Santa Trìnita** was rebuilt in Gothic style in the 14th century, before a Baroque facade was added in the 1590s by Buontalenti. On the east wall there are traces of the former Romanesque church.

The altarpiece, called the *The Adoration of the Shepherds*, was painted in 1485 by Domenico Ghirlandaio, who managed to squeeze in a self-portrait in the figure of the first shepherd. He also painted the exquisite series of frescoes in the Cappella Sassetti, to the right of the altar, which show the church in the 1480s.

On the other side of the altar is Luca della Robbia's impressive marble tomb of Benozzo Federighi.

Santa Trìnita

Piazza di Santa Trìnita
☎ 055 216-912
🕐 Mon-Sun: 7am-12noon & 4pm-7pm.

18 · Exploring Florence: Central Florence

The largest and most magnificent Renaissance palace in town, **Palazzo Strozzi**, was built by the powerful banker, and rival to the Medicis, Filippo Strozzi. He demolished more than 15 buildings in 1489 to create this monument to his wealth. Filippo died in 1491, leaving his heirs to finish building. Construction was finally completed in 1536, by which time the family was bankrupt.

Palazzo Strozzi

Piazza degli Strozzi
🕐 Opening times depend on exhibitions.

The palace today is an exhibition centre and home to various cultural institutes, with a small museum tracing the building's history in pictures and models.

The heavily fortified **Palazzo Spini-Ferroni** was built in the 1290s to guard the Santa Trìnita bridge, and was the town hall from 1865 to 1871.

The building now houses the Salvatore Ferragamo shoe shop and a small museum, the **Museo Ferragamo**, dedicated to his designs. Ferragamo was born in 1898 near Naples and emigrated to the US in 1914 to work on movies. In 1927 he moved to Florence and opened his shop, catering for the likes of Audrey Hepburn and Lauren Bacall. *(Via Tirbabuoni 2, ☎ 055 336-0456. 🕐 Mon-Fri: 9am-1pm & 2-6pm.)*

The small church of **Santi Apostoli** was said to be founded by Charlemagne, but probably dates from the 1050s, still making it one of the oldest in Florence.

Orsanmichele

Behind its simple Romanesque facade, it has the structure of a Roman basilica – a rectangle with a flat roof. The most interesting features inside the church are its relics, including stone fragments reputedly brought from the Holy

Exploring Florence: Central Florence · 19

Sepulchre in Jerusalem. The church lies on land that was once a cemetery for infants who died before being baptised. *(Piazza del Limbo, ☎ 055 290-642. ◷ Mon-Sun: 10am-12noon & 3.30pm-6.30pm.)*

The austere 14th-century **Palazzo Davanzati** – note the thick gates and the openings in the courtyard where molten lead was poured over invaders – was acquired by the Davanzatis in 1578. Their coat of arms graces the narrow five-storey facade.

Today it houses the **Museo della Casa Fiorentina Antica** (Museum of Domestic Florence), which recreates life in a wealthy 15th-century family home. Art collector Elia Volpi bought, restored and opened the palazzo to the public in 1986, faithfully installing elaborate wall hangings and plush furnishings from the period.

Among the museum's more interesting items are a 15th-century toilet, top-floor kitchen with dumb waiter, and the magnificent parrot motifs of the Sala dei Pappagalli. The museum also features an exhibition of European lace from the 16th to the 19th centuries.

In a stone loggia from the 1540s, the so-called **Mercato Nuovo** (New Market) once traded in fine material but now operates for the benefit of tourists, trading mostly in leather goods, cheap silk scarves and souvenirs. It is known locally as Il Porcellino, after the fountain to the south featuring a bronze statue of a boar (the original is in the Uffizi). Put a coin in its mouth for good luck and rub his nose to ensure you return to Florence.

Built in 1290 by Cambio as a loggia to house the city's grain market, the open arcades of **Orsanmichele** were bricked up and the building was turned into a church in the 1360s. Orsanmichele then became the church of the Arts. Different guilds vied to have the best statue of their patron saint. These figures are displayed in 14 niches on the facades, creating an impressive outdoor sculpture gallery.

The roll-call is impressive: Ghiberti's *St. John the Baptist*, Verrochio's *Incredulity of St. Thomas*, Giambologna's *St. Luke* and

Palazzo Davanzati Museo della Casa Fiorentina Antica

Via Porta Rossa 13
☎ 055 238-8610
◷ Tue-Sat: 8.30am-12.50pm.
Currently closed for restoration (except loggia).

Mercato Nuovo

Piazza Mercato Nuovo
◷ Apr-Oct: Mon-Sun: 9am-7pm. Nov-Mar: Tue-Sat: 9am-7pm.

Orsanmichele

Via Arte della Lana
☎ 055 284-715
◷ Mon-Sun: 9am-12noon & 4pm-6pm.

20 · Exploring Florence: Central Florence

The fountain of Neptune, Piazza della Signorina

Donatello's *St. Peter* and *St. Mark* are among the cream of Italian art produced in the 15th and 16th centuries.

Inside, the church is decorated with 14th-century frescoes depicting scenes from the Old and New Testaments. Andrea Orcagna's tabernacle on the right of the nave is a feast of carved cherubs and inlaid marble, an intricate Gothic masterpiece from the 1350s.

Santo Stefano al Ponte (Saint Stephen by the Bridge) has stood close to the Ponte Vecchio since 969, although the current Romanesque-style building dates from the 1230s.

The green and white marble striped facade is a Gothic addition, apart from the original lower part. The interior was decorated in the Baroque style in the mid-17th century, with a 16th-century high altar by Giambologna and a staircase by Buontalenti, both taken from other churches.

Today, the deconsecrated church is home to the Orchestra Regionale Toscana, and hosts regular orchestral concerts.

The Renaissance is usually seen in terms of artists and architects. The fine **Museo di Storia della Scienza** (Museum of the History of Science) redresses the balance with displays of scientific instruments from the Accademia del Cimento, an

Santo Stefano al Ponte

Piazza Santo Stefano al Ponte.
◐ Open during concerts.

Exploring Florence: Central Florence · 21

experimental establishment set up in the 1650s. The museum's core exhibits were amassed by the Medicis in the 16th and 17th centuries, and by the house of Lorraine during the 18th century.

Galileo Galilei's collection of telescopes and lenses is the star exhibit here, along with reconstructions of some of his experiments and, oddly, a bone from his finger. Ground-breaking nautical instruments, astronomic and terrestrial clocks and Portuguese cartographer Lopo Homen's map of the world (1554) are among the other fascinating exhibits.

The ancient herbalist shop, **Eboristeria**, is just off Piazza della Signoria. It is decorated inside with medieval frescoes and sells soap, pot-pourri, fragrances and cosmetics made using the traditional methods of various religious orders throughout Tuscany.

To ease the crowded city streets, the **Piazza della Signoria** was constructed in the 1320s by clearing away the homes of disgraced local families. The city's population has traditionally gathered here for *parlementos* (public meetings), parades, celebrations of major events, to welcome visiting dignitaries and to protest. The religious fanatic Girolamo Savonarola was burnt at the stake here in 1498.

The irregular space is cleverly filled by statues, deftly positioned here in the mid-16th century when the square was turned into an outdoor sculpture gallery. The focus is Bartolomeo Ammannati's *Fonte del Nettuno* of 1575, which is artfully surrounded by Giambologna's superb water nymphs.

Everyone crowds around the copy of Michelangelo's *David*, the original of which is in the Accademia (page 38). The original was sculpted in 1501 to honour the Florentine Republic's triumph over Medici tyranny. Either side of it are copies of Donatello's *Marzocco* (the original of which is in the Bargello, page 26), the city's emblematic lion, and his *Judith and Holofernes* (the original of which is in the Palazzio Vecchio, page 22). Last in line is *Hercules and Cacus* by Bandinelli.

Museo di Storia della Scienza

Piazza dei Guidici 1
☎ 055 239-8876
🕒 Mon, Wed & Fri: 9.30am-1pm & 2pm-5pm. Tue, Thu & Sat: 9.30am-1pm. Sun: closed.

Eboristeria

Via Vaccherecchia 9r
☎ 055 239-6055
🕒 Tue-Sat: 9am-7.30pm. Sun-Mon: closed.

Piazza della Signoria

22 · Exploring Florence: Central Florence

Michelangelo's David in the Piazza della Signorina

The Loggia di Lanzi of 1382, named after Cosimo's lancers (bodyguards), showcases more sculpture. Cellini's bronze *Perseus* holds up Medusa's head, while Giambologna's *Rape of the Sabine Women* is a masterpiece of twisting figures. Giambologna was also responsible for the impressive bronze equestrian figure of Cosimo I in the middle of the square.

The **Palazzo della Cassa di Risparmio** is home to the **Raccolta di Arte Contemporanea "Alberto della Ragione"**, a collection of modern national art. It is named after the Genoese merchant Alberto Della Ragione, who donated his priceless collection of art to the city in 1970.

The 21 rooms are devoted to 20th-century Italian artists and sculptors. It charts the development of modern Italian art through Futurism to Metaphysical Art and beyond. Artists represented here include Marino Marini, De Chirico, Morandi, Casorati and De Pisis. Works from the Roman School, which included Scipione and Mafai, can also be seen.

Begun in 1299 by Arnolfo di Cambio to house the *Priori*, or magistrates, of the Commune, the **Palazzo Vecchio** still serves as the city's town hall after almost 700 years. The Medicis took up residence in 1540 and commissioned Giorgio Vasari to remodel the building. Adding a huge extension on the back, he turned it into the city's most lavish palace.

You enter via an enclosed courtyard, whose frescoed walls show views of the Hapsburg Empire. The huge Salone dei

Raccolta di Arte Contemporanea "Alberto della ragione"

Piazza della Signoria 5
☎ 055 283 078
⏲ Mon & Wed-Sat: 8.30am-1.30pm. Sun: 8am-1pm. Tue: closed. Admission charge.
Musei Fiorentini discount – 2 carnets for the price of 1 (carnet comprises 10 coupons for 50% discount on admission to participating museums and galleries) with voucher on page 71.

Exploring Florence: Central Florence · 23

Cinquento, the assembly hall for the Great Council and the Medicis' audience chamber, is covered with heroic battle scenes by Vasari – but the room's prime exhibit is Michelangelo's *Victory*, intended for the tomb of Pope Julius II.

The second floor offers yet more splendour, including a suite of rooms dedicated to pagan gods. The tiny Cappella di Eleanora decorated by Bronzino, the Sala dei Gigli named after the gold lilies on its walls, Ghirlandaio's frescoes of Roman statesmen, and a fabulous ceiling by the Maiano brothers are just some of the many highlights.

From the Sala d'Udienza, you can sometimes climb to the top of the palace's distinctive 94-metre (300-foot) tower, past a prison cell where numerous traitors to the Republic were kept.

Palazzo Vecchio

Piazza della Signoria
☎ 055 276-8465
🕑 Mon-Wed, Fri & Sat: 9am-7pm. Thu: 9am-2pm. Sun: 8am-1pm. Admission charge.
Musei Fiorentini discount – 2 carnets for the price of 1 (carnet comprises 10 coupons for 50% discount on admission to participating museums and galleries) with voucher on page 71.

The **Palazzo degli Uffizi** was built around three sides of a courtyard as offices, or *uffizi*, to administer the whole of Tuscany in 1560. Designed by Vasari, the four-storey complex symbolically cowers beneath the bulk of the ruling Palazzo Vecchio. The Uffizi was connected to another Medici palace, the **Palazzo Pitti** (page 42), by a long corridor leading over the Ponte Vecchio, so members of the ruling family could move around Florence without having to mix with the city's ordinary people.

From as early as the 1580s, the Medicis

Palazzo Vecchio

24 · Exploring Florence: Central Florence

Uffizi

Uffizi

Loggiato degli Uffizi 6
☎ 055 238-85
🕒 Tue-Sun: 8.30am-7pm. Mon: closed.
Admission charge.

used the upper floor to display their art collection, making the Uffizi the oldest gallery in the world. Bequeathed to the nation in 1737, the 4,000 works on a single floor make the gallery more intimate than many other collections of a comparable size.

Entering from the Piazza della Signoria end of the building, you pass through an antique sculpture gallery, which displays pieces used as sources of inspiration by Renaissance artists. The tail-end of Tuscan Gothic art is represented by the late 13th-century *Maestà* and the early 14th-century *Ognissanti Madonna* by Giotto, whose naturalism revolutionised painting.

Three rooms are devoted to the early Renaissance masters. Among the paintings on display are the *Battle of San Romano* by Uccello, Piero della Francesca's companion portraits of the *Duke* and *Duchess of Urbino*, and Fra Filippo Lippi's *Madonna and Child*.

The highlights of the gallery, Botticelli's works, are spread over five rooms. They include his famous masterpieces from the 1470s and 80s – *The Birth of Venus*, *The Adoration of the Magi* and *Primavera*. Examples of Leonardo's early works are displayed in a single room – *The Annunciation* and *Adoration of the Magi*. The High Renaissance of the early 1500s is represented by Michelangelo's *Holy Family*, Bronzino's *Madonna*, Raphael's *Madonna of the Goldfinch* and Titian's *Urbino Venus*.

The long corridor overlooking the River Arno is a showcase of Roman statuary collected by the Medici in the 15th

Exploring Florence: Central Florence · 25

century. The later paintings, which are arranged in the west wing, include works by Caravaggio, Rubens, Rembrandt and Van Dyck.

Badia Fiorentina, an ancient Benedictine abbey opposite the Bargello (page 26), which treated the sick, was the richest medieval religious foundation in Florence. It was founded in 978 and rebuilt by Cambio in 1330.

Inside, the most interesting features are Filippino Lippi's depiction of the *Madonna and St. Bernard*, left of the entrance door, and Mino da Fiesole's monument to Ugo of Tuscany, the founder's son.

A narrow staircase from the choir leads to the beautiful two-storey Chiostro degli Arranci, where the Benedictine monks once grew orange trees. There are still 15th-century frescoes of the life of St. Benedict on the upper storey, and an early fresco by Bronzino (1503–72) in the north walkway.

The church also has historical connections. The poet Boccaccio delivered lectures about Dante's work here in the 14th century, and Dante himself conceived his lifelong passion for Beatrice in these aisles – although she was married to someone else soon after.

Dante may well have been born in the **Casa di Dante** in 1265, although it can't be proved. Still, the author of *The Divine Comedy*, who is recognised as the lynchpin of Italian literature, is honoured here with a museum dedicated solely to his life and work.

Built in the 13th century, the house is a rambling maze of small rooms filled with

Badia Fiorentina

Via del Proconsolo
Mon-Sat: 4.30am-6.30pm. Sun: 10.30am-11.30am.

Badia Fiorentina

26 · Exploring Florence: Central Florence

facsimiles of archive material, copies of his works in various languages, and documents pertaining to Florence at the time that the great writer lived. The ground floor also plays host to exhibitions of modern paintings and sculpture.

Michelangelo lived in at least two of the five houses that stood on the **Casa Buonarroti** site. The lovely 17th-century building that remains today is home to a priceless collection of his work, an idea conceived in 1612 by his great-nephew, Michelangelo Buonarroti the Younger.

The collection has an especially good selection of Michelangelo's earlier works, with a marble relief of the *Madonna della Scala (1490*–92), produced when he was just 16, and the unfinished *Battle of the Centaurs* (1492). Both sculptures reveal the influence of Donatello on the young artist.

Other works include the unused wooden model for the San Lorenzo facade that Michelangelo designed, a wooden crucifix, said to be an immature work, and the torso of a river god destined for the Medici church of San Lorenzo (page 31).

As well as Michelangelo's work, the collection includes pieces by artists from several different periods. There are some beautiful frescoes by Jacopo Vignali that date from 1622, and a bust of Michelangelo by his close friend Daniele da Volterra.

The museum also contains a priceless archaeological collection amassed by Filippo Buonnarroti in the 18th century. It is made up of Etruscan remains found in the vicinity of Florence.

One of Florence's foremost museums, the **Museo Nazionale del Bargello**, occupies what was once the city's town hall, a heavily fortified building dating from 1250 that had been used as law courts, a prison, torture rooms and the residence of the chief of police. Criminals and political enemies were once executed in the courtyard.

In 1859 it became a national museum, devoted to Florentine Renaissance

---

Casa di Dante

Via Santa Margherita 1
☎ 055 219-416
⊕ Mar-Oct: Mon & Wed-Sat: 10am-6pm Sun: 10am-2pm. Tue: closed. Nov-Mar: Mon & Wed-Sat: 10am-4pm Sun: 10am-2pm. Tue: closed.
Admission charge.

Casa Buonarroti

Via Ghibellina 70
☎ 055 241-752
⊕ Wed-Mon: 9.30am-1.30pm. Tue: closed.
Admission charge.
2 admissions for the price of 1 with voucher on page 69.

Exploring Florence: Central Florence · 27

sculpture. Today, it is the most illuminating, visually exciting and important collection of its kind in the world.

The first room is dominated by Michelangelo. The highlights are his bibulous marble *Bacchus*, the unfinished relief called the *Tondo Pitti* and his bust of *Brutus*, which is supposedly modelled on one of the Medici clan.

Works of his followers – notably Cellini and Sansovino – pale in comparison, apart from the famous athletic *Winged Mercury* of 1564 by Giambologna.

The first floor is reached by the loggia, where Giambologna's bronze birds are the dominant feature. Works spanning Donatello's entire life include the bronze *David* from the 1430s and his superbly tense *St. George* from the facade of Orsanmichele. Entries for the competition of 1401 to design the Baptistery doors – notably by Ghiberti and Brunelleschi – show the first developments of Renaissance art.

The second floor houses a collection of arms and armour, including an exquisite inlaid ivory saddle made for the Medici in the 15th century, and a room of small bronzes. An absolute must is Verrochio's serene *Lady with a Posy*, clearly inspired by his master, Leonardo da Vinci.

The Franciscan church of **Santa Croce**, which was supposedly founded by St. Francis himself, was started in 1294 by Cambio and intended to be the largest church in the

Museo Nazionale del Bargello

Via del Proconsolo 4
☎ 055 238-8606
⏲ Tue-Sat: 8.30am-1.50pm. Open alternate Mondays and Sundays. Admission charge.

Casa Buonarroti

28 · Exploring Florence: Central Florence

Santa Croce

Piazza Santa Croce
☎ 055 244-619
⏲ Apr-Sep: Mon-Sat:
8am-6.30pm. Sun: 3pm-
6pm. Oct-Mar: Mon-Sat
8am-12.30pm & 3pm-
6.30pm. Sun 3pm-6pm.

Museo dell'Opera di Santa Croce

☎ 055 244-619

Christian world. It is without doubt the richest medieval church in Florence, with a staggering collection of frescoes and many magnificent tombs – despite the order's vow of poverty.

Behind the 1860s' Neo-Gothic facade, the interior is dimly lit and gloomy, but it is also Florence's mostly richly decorated. Almost 300 tombstones make up the floor of the nave, and many of the great and good are buried here. Michelangelo's tomb is on the right. Carved by Vasari, it appropriately features the figures of Painting, Architecture and Sculpture.

Galileo's, opposite, was not carved until the 1730s – he was condemned by the Church for his heretical research in 1616 and was only given a Christian burial in 1737, a total of 95 years after his death. Next to Michelangelo, Dante is honoured by a memorial but is buried in Ravenna. Further along, Machiavelli took his place here in 1527.

The chancel has murals and stained glass by Agnolo Gaddi, dating from the 1390s. The chapels around the altar feature yet more masterpieces. To the right, in the Perruzi and Bardi chapels, are some Giotto frescoes from the early 14th century – the Bardi Chapel's scenes from the life of St. Francis are especially noteworthy, along with a wooden crucifix by Donatello. On the far left of the church is the Baroque Niccolini Chapel, with its frescoes by Volterrano completed in the 1580s.

To the right of the altar is a complex of rooms. The Sacristy has a marvellous crucifix by Giotto's pupil Taddeo Gaddi, who also executed the frescoes in the adjoining Cappella Rinuccini. The Cappella Medici is rarely open but has a fine altarpiece, and the Baroncelli Chapel has the first frescoed night scenes, depicting angels appearing to sleeping shepherds (1338), also by Taddeo Gaddi.

The **Museo dell'Opera di Santa Croce** contains an interesting collection of treasures, including Cimabue's *Crucifixion*, which was badly damaged in the flood, Taddeo Gaddi's *Last Supper* from 1340, and Donatello's *St. Louis of Toulouse*,

Exploring Florence: Central Florence · 29

which was originally from Orsanmichele (page 19). It is also the workshop that restores works of art, many of which were damaged in the 1966 flood that submerged the church in over 6 metres (20 feet) of water.

Off the north side of the large first cloister is the masterpiece **Cappella dei Pazzi**, an intimate family chapel. Designed by Brunelleschi in 1429, this exquisite room's

Santa Croce

proportions are based on a square and a circle. The domed ceiling has terracotta roundels by Luca della Robbia. Beyond it is the second cloister – the city's most beautiful – probably built by Rossellino in the 1450s.

The **Palazzo Corsi-Alberti** was built in the 15th century and since 1922 it has been open to the public as the **Museo della Fondazione H.P. Horne**. This collection of art, sculpture, ceramics, objets d'art and furniture was accumulated by Herbert Percy Horne. This English architect and art historian purchased the palace at the end of the 19th century and bequeathed it to the state upon his death. The value of his legacy lies in his successful recreation of a Florentine Renaissance home, complete with authentic art, furnishings and fabrics.

In the 16th century, when the palace was

Cappella dei Pazzi

Piazza di Santa Croce 16
☎ 055 244-619
🕐 Apr-Sep: Mon, Tue & Thu-Sun: 10am-12.30pm & 2.30pm-6.30pm. Oct-Mar: Mon & Tue, Thu-Sun: 10am-12noon & 3pm-5pm. Wed: closed. Admission charge.

30 · Exploring Florence: Central Florence

Saint Stephen, Museo Horne

owned by the silk manufacturing Alberti family, the ground floor was used for dyeing and storage purposes. Today it displays such treasures as a Roman sarcophagus dating from the 4th century and Sienese furniture from the 17th century. There are also interesting collections of coins and ceramics.

The main room on the first floor, which would have been the family's dining room, displays *Shepherd's Adoration* by Correggio, *Allegory of Music* by Dosso Dossi and works by Signorelli, Donatello, Lorenzetti, Lippi and di Cristofano, as well as some precious pieces of 16th- and 17th-century furniture.

The **Wife's Chamber** is home to one of the highlights of the museum, Giotto's *St. Stephen*. Horne purchased this, not in Florence, but from an antique shop in London. It would originally have formed one of several panels and dates from about 1317. Also in this room are Ceccarelli's *Madonna and Child* and *Lot's Wife* by Furini.

The **Husband's Chamber**, connected to the wife's by a corridor, contains Taddeo Gaddi's *Madonna with the Child* and *The Face of the Redeemer*. There is also an exquisite tapestry dating back to the 15th century, and some Tuscan religious artefacts.

The kitchen displays a notable collection of Renaissance utensils made by German artisans in the city, including a fine coffee grinder.

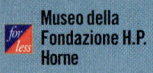
Museo della Fondazione H.P. Horne

Via dei Benci 6
☎ 055 244-6 61
◷ Mon-Sat: 9am-1pm.
Sun: closed.
Admission charge.
2 admissions for the price of 1 with voucher on page 71.

Northern Florence

The 11th-century Romanesque **San Lorenzo** was the Medicis' own parish church. Brunelleschi was commissioned to rebuild it in 1419, resulting in today's masterpiece of Renaissance design.

The nave contains several priceless works, including a pair of pulpits with exquisite bronze scenes of *Christ's Passion* and *Resurrection* by Donatello. The fundamentalist Savonarola delivered his heated sermons from here. Also noteworthy is Bronzino's decadent depiction of the *Martyrdom of St. Lawrence*, on the left side of the nave.

The true glories of the church lie outside the nave. Behind the high altar is the monumentally gloomy Cappella dei Principi of 1604, constructed as the mausoleum of six members of the Medici family. The heavy marble decoration by Matteo Nigetti incorporated precious stones produced by the newly established Opificio delle Pietre Dure (page 37).

Next door, the Old Sacristy was built by Brunelleschi in the 1420s, the first chapel to base its proportions on a perfect cube. The decorations by Donatello include fine bronze doors, a fresco of the Florence skyline at night and statues of various Medici princes.

The New Sacristy is dominated by the tombs of two Medici princes designed by Michelangelo. These feature the figures of Dawn and Dusk and of Night and Day, each a masterpiece of execution. Some original sketches by Michelangelo kept behind the altar can also be viewed on a free tour.

Michelangelo's involvement can also be seen in the design of the Biblioteca Medicea Laurenziana, to the left of the nave, built to house the Medici manuscript collection. Michelangelo designed everything from the dramatic sandstone staircase leading up to the large rectangular room, to the desks, ceiling and bookcases.

In the shadow of the large dome of San Lorenzo's Cappella dei Principi, which

San Lorenzo

Piazza di San Lorenzo
☎ 055 216-634
🕘 Church:
Mon-Sun: 7am-12noon & 3.30pm-6.30pm.
Library:
Mon-Sat: 9am-2pm. Sun: closed.
Medici chapels:
Tue-Sat: 8.30am-5pm.
Sun: 8.30am-3.30pm.
Mon: closed.

32 · Exploring Florence: Northern Florence

San Lorenzo

Palazzo Medici Riccardi

Via Cavour 1
⊕ Mon-Sat: 9am-1pm.
Sun: 9am-12noon.
Chapel:
⊕ Mon-Tue & Thu-Sat: 9am-1pm & 3pm-6pm.
Sun: 9am-1pm. Wed: closed.

Palazzo Pucci

Via de' Pucci 6
☎ 055 283-061
⊕ Accessories showroom open by appointment only.

echoes that of the Duomo (page 10) – the **Piazza di San Lorenzo** is dominated by the church's unfinished brick facade. In 1518 Michelangelo's marble design was rejected, as it was considered far too flamboyant you can see a model of it in the Casa Buonarroti (page 26).

Near the entrance to the church is a statue of Giovanni delle Bande Nere, the first Medici duke, which was cast by Baccio Bandinelli in 1540.

The **Palazzo Medici Riccardi** was the family home of the Medicis for one hundred years until their move to the Palazzo Vecchio (page 22) in 1540. This austere palazzo was built for Cosimo I by Michelozzo. Its rusticated first storey gives away nothing of the opulence that the family enjoyed inside.

The palace-fortress was widely copied in its time, although the open arches have since been bricked up and windows were added by Michelangelo. The palazzo was greatly expanded when the Riccardi family took up residence in 1659.

Today, the courtyard forms an outdoor sculpture gallery, with Roman statuary and fragments, and Bandinelli's statue of Orpheus. Just two rooms are open to the public – the Luca Giordano Room, named after the Baroque artist who painted its walls and ceiling in the 1680s, and the Cappella dei Magi, with its vibrant fresco of the *Procession of the Magi* by Benozzo Gozzoli from the 1450s.

The **Palazzo Pucci** was the ancestral home of the Puccis, staunch allies of the Medicis, and was designed by Ammannati in the 16th century. Haute couture

Exploring Florence: Northern Florence · 33

designer Emilio Pucci has a boutique in the nearby Via della Vigna Nuova.

The facade was added in the 1650s – note the coat of arms of Leo X on the corner of the Via dei Servi by Bacio da Montelupo.

Despite the rather erratic labelling of its exhibits, the **Museo di Firenze com'era** (Florence As It Was Museum) is an absorbing collection of maps, models, photographs, documents, prints and paintings showing the city's development from the Renaissance to the 19th century.

Contained within the 15th-century Convento delle Oblate, the museum houses the original plans of city architect Guiseppe Poggi, who proposed bulldozing much of the medieval city in the 1860s to create a worthy capital for Italy – fortunately only the area around the present **Piazza della Repubblica** was flattened.

Also in the collection are the 12 famous lunettes by the Flemish artist Giusto Utens. They feature views of the Medici villas in 1599, as well as a 19th-century copy of a 1470 woodcut panorama of the city, the *Pianta della Catena*, one of the collection's most illuminating exhibits. The two obvious omissions from the panel are the Uffizi and Pitti palaces, neither of which had then been built. The first topographical map of the city, attributed to Stefano Bonsignori and dating from 1594, can also be seen.

The 18th century is documented in a series of views of Florence by Zocchi, and the 19th-century paintings include studies of the Jewish Ghetto and the Mercato

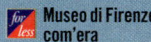
Museo di Firenze com'era

Via dell'Oriuolo 24
☎ 055 261-6545
🕐 Mon-Wed, Fri & Sat: 9am-2pm. Sun: 8am-1pm. Thu: closed.
Admission charge.
Musei Fiorentini discount - 2 carnets for the price of 1 (carnet comprises 10 coupons for 50% discount on admission to participating museums and galleries) with voucher on page 71.

Interior of San Lorenzo

34 · Exploring Florence: Northern Florence

Museo Archeologico

Via della Colonna 38
☎ 055 23-575
⏲ Tue-Sat: 9am-2pm.
Sun: 9am-1pm. Mon: closed.
Admission charge.

Santa Maria Maddelena dei Pazzi

Borgo Pinti 58
☎ 055 247-8420
⏲ Mon-Sun: 9am-12noon & 5pm-7pm.

Museo Ebraico

Via Farini 4
☎ 055 245-252
⏲ Sun-Thu: 10am-1pm & 2pm-5pm. Fri: 10am-1pm. Sat: closed.

Vecchio before they were demolished.

A new exhibition, *Alle origini di Firenze* (The Origins of Florence), goes still further back in time to document the development of the Florentine area from the time of the first settlers through to the ancient Roman period.

One of Florence's most fascinating collections is housed in the **Palazzo della Crocetta**, built for Medici princess Maria Maddalena in 1620. The **Museo Archeologico** (Archaeological Museum) is based on bequests from the Lorraine and Medici families.

The Etruscan treasures are the most absorbing, with an array of kitchen utensils, funerary urns and bronze jewellery, as well as the famous 5th-century BC bronze *Chimera* and the *Arrigatore*, a bronze Roman Orator from the 1st century BC. Several sarcophogi complete the exhibits – that of the Fat Man in alabaster and the Amazons in marble.

The Greek world is represented by various statues and fragments. The 5th-century BC horse's head, the *Idolino*, and the so-called François vase, a vase covered in mythological figures found in an Etruscan tomb, are both outstanding. The highlight within the Egyptian collection is a 14th-century BC Hittite chariot of bone and wood.

Named after the revolt of the city's dyers and wool workers in 1378, the **Piazza dei Ciompi**'s main feature is the graceful loggia built by Casari in 1568 for Mercato Vecchio. The market building was originally on the site of the Piazza Repubblica and was dismantled in the 1860s during Poggi's mass destruction and replanning of the area.

The 13th-century Cistercian convent of **Santa Maria Maddelena dei Pazzi** was rebuilt by Sangallo in the 1480s. The church originally contained an impressive collection of works of art, including examples by Botticelli, Ghirlandaio and Perugino, which have since been distributed to other museums.

Exploring Florence: Northern Florence · 35

Piazza dei Ciompi

The church itself is not the main attraction, even though its Roman Baroque interior is considered the finest in town and contains a crucifix by the young Buontalenti. The chapter house, entered through the underground crypt, is the reason people visit here. It contains a famous series of frescoes painted by Perugino and his assistants during the 1490s.

Covering an entire wall, Perugino's *Crucifixion* is seen as if viewed through the open arches of a loggia, with a harmonious, idyllic landscape turning the horror of the Crucifixion into a pleasant pastoral scene.

When the **Piazza della Repubblica** was created in the 1860s, most of the city's Jewish ghetto was cleared. In 1874, the huge **Tempio Israelitico** (Synagogue) was built in Spanish-Moorish style.

Next to the synagogue is the **Museo Ebraico di Firenze**, a small museum of Jewish ritual objects dating back to the 17th century.

The 14th-century church of **San Marco** was rebuilt by Michelozzi in the following century, when Dominican monks from nearby Fiesole moved here under the patronage of Cosimo il Vecchio.

The church contains Fra' Angelico's crucifix for the main altar, which dates from the 1420s, and Fra' Bartolomeo's exquisite *Virgin and Saints* on the right-

San Marco

Piazza di San Marco
☎ 055 238-8608
⏲ Tue-Sat: 8.30am-1.50pm. Open alternate Mondays and Sundays. Admission charge.

36 · Exploring Florence: Northern Florence

San Marco

hand side of the nave. The complex is most famous for the series of devotional frescoes painted in the monks' dormitories by resident Fra' Angelico.

The cloister now holds a small museum, containing Fra' Angelico's *Deposition*, a moving scene of the Virgin Mary cradling the dead Christ. There is also his famous San Marco altarpiece and *Last Judgment*. In the chapter house opposite is his moving *Crucifixion* (1441–42).

Upstairs are the spartan dormitory cells. At the top of the staircase is the celebrated *Annunciation*, set in a Florentine loggia, opposite a *Crucifix with St. Dominic*. The cells contain 35 scenes from the life of Christ painted almost single-handedly by Fra' Angelico. Cell 2 contains the moving *Entombment*, Cell 4 the *Crucifixion*, Cell 7 the painful *Mocking of Christ*, Cell 25 *Our Lady of the Shadows*, Cell 34 *Christ Praying in the Garden*, and Cell 39 *The Adoration of the Magi*.

Cells 12 to 14 contain artefacts from the life of the fanatical Savonarola, one-time prior of the convent, including a portrait of him as St. Peter by Fra' Bartolomeo. Michelozzo also built Europe's first public library here in 1441. A light and airy room, it was intended to house the Medici's Greek and Latin tomes.

Giardino dei Semplici

Via Micheli 3
☎ 055 275-7402
⏲ Mon & Wed: 9am–12noon & 2.30pm–5pm. Fri: 9am–12noon. Tue, Thu, Sat & Sun: closed.

Built by Niccolo Tribolo on land seized from the Dominican order in 1545, the so-called **Giardino dei Semplici** (Garden of Simples) still retains its original layout. It was planted for Cosimo I to grow herbs and plants, both for medicinal purposes and the extraction of essential oils. It now also contains tropical plants.

Exploring Florence: Northern Florence · 37

The small museums dotted throughout the grounds include a gallery of mineralogy, a geology collection with some interesting fossils, and an exhibition showing the specimens of rare plants.

Michelozzo's opulent design of **Santissima Annunziata** in the 1440s replaced an earlier church of the order. Its interior was later remodelled in Baroque style.

The atrium contains a cycle of frescoes, the finest being Andrea del Sarto's *Journey of the Magi* and *Birth of the Virgin*. In the nave, the *Virgin Mary* was painted by a monk – and supposedly finished by angels in the 1250s. Andrea del Sarto also painted the *Head of Christ* in the nave, and the masterpiece *Madonna del Sacco* fresco in the 1520s.

One of the earliest examples of urban planning in Florence, the harmonious **Piazza Santissima Annunziata** is surrounded on three sides by arcades. Brunelleschi built the Spedale degli Innocenti in 1419, and when Antonio da Sangallo cleared the area in 1519, he echoed the hospital's facade opposite in the Confraternita dei Servi di Maria. The theme was continued when the church's portico was rebuilt in 1601.

Opened in 1444, the first foundling hospital in Europe, **Spedale degli Innocenti**, was designed by Brunelleschi in 1419 as part of a projected square that was only finished in the 17th century. Adorned with light blue roundels of infants by della Robbia, the portico features a rotating device so mothers with unwanted children could leave their babies anonymously.

Upstairs, there is a collection of frescoes by Florentine masters, and the **Pinacoteca dello Spedal**, an exhibition of paintings, sculptures, miniatures and furniture from the 14th to the 18th century. It contains Botticelli's *Virgin Mary with the Christ Child* and Ghirlandaio's *Adoration of the Magi*.

Grand Duke Ferdinanddo I de' Medici founded the **Opificio e Museo delle Pietre Dure** (Factory of Precious Stones) in 1588 to decorate the gloomy mausoleum in the

---

Santissima Annunziata

Piazza della Santissima Annunziata
☎ 055 239-8034
⊕ Mon-Sat: 6.30am-12.30pm & 4pm-7.30pm. Sun: 8.30am-12.30pm & 4pm-9pm.

Spedale degli Innocenti

Piazza della Santissima Annunziata 12
☎ 055 249-1708
⊕ Thu-Tue: 8.30am-2pm. Wed: closed.
Admission charge.

Opificio delle Pietre Dure

Via degli Alfani 78
☎ 055 265-111
⊕ Mon-Sat: 9am-2pm.
Sun: closed.
Admission charge.

38 · Exploring Florence: Northern Florence

Statue of David in the Galleria dell'Accademia

Galleria dell'Accademia

Via Ricasoli 60
☎ 055 238-8609
🕒 Tue-Sun: 8.30am-6.50pm. Mon: closed.
Admission charge.

Cenacolo di Sant'Apollonia

Via XXVII Aprile 1
☎ 055 238-8607
🕒 Tue-Sat: 8.30am-1.50pm. Open alternate Mondays and Sundays.

church of San Lorenzo with inlays of semi-precious stones. Today, the factory is housed in the former monastery of San Niccolò and mainly carries out restoration work.

The small museum contains a selection of table tops inlaid with marble and stones, portraits and vases – including one inlaid with a harp by Zocchi in 1849 – as well as tools and workbenches.

Florence's music academy, the **Conservatorio Musicale Luigi Cherubini**, is named after a 19th-century Florentine composer, and was set up at the beginning of the 19th century. Today it has one of the country's best music libraries, with original manuscripts by Rossini and Monteverdi, as well as a collection of musical instruments, including several Stradivarius violins. Unfortunately, it is not open to the public without special permission.

The **Galleria dell'Accademia** (Academy of Fine Arts) was founded in 1563 as the first school in Europe to teach the techniques of painting, sculpture and architecture. In 1784, an art collection was established to give students models to work from. By the time Michelangelo's works were bequeathed in 1873, the collection was renowned.

It is the statue of *David* (1504) that the crowds flock to. Carved from a single block of marble when the sculptor was just 29, the carving of this nude biblical hero was commissioned by the city in order that a great work should stand in the Piazza della Signoria. Other works by Michelangelo include the unfinished *Prisoners* (1519–1536) for the tomb of Julius II, which he abandoned to paint the Sistine Chapel.

Exploring Florence: Northern Florence · 39

Also worthy of a detour are Fra Bartolomeo's *St. Catherine*, Filippino Lippi's *Deposition from the Cross*, Monaco's *Annunciation*, and Botticelli's *Madonna of the Sea*. Paintings include the Byzantine collection of pre-Giotto paintings, with several key works by Uccello.

All that remains of the Benedictine convent **Cenacolo di Sant'Apollonia** is a cloister and the refectory, now used by students of Florence University. Andrea del Castagno's masterpiece frescoes cover the main wall of the refectory. The pupil of the great Masaccio worked here in the 1440s, producing a series of moving and sometimes shocking images in the *Last Supper*, *Resurrection*, *Crucifixion* and *Deposition*.

Also known as the Fortezza di San Giovanni, the **Fortezza da Basso** (Lower Fort) – as opposed to the hilltop Forte di Belvedere across the river – covers a vast area next to the railway station. To protect the city against both outside invaders and civic uprisings, Duke Alessandro de' Medici commissioned Antonio da Sangallo to build this stronghold in 1534. Constructed in the shape of a pentagon with 12-metre (40-foot) high walls, the fort contains a vast octagonal guard room with an impressive dome.

The **Museo Stibbert** is situated yet further north but is definitely worth a trip. The eclectic collection of arms, armour, costumes and furnishings was put together in the latter part of the 19th century by Frederick Stibbert, an eccentric of English descent.

The 50,000 items are displayed in the renovated Villa di Montughi, which has been decorated in the style of the 15th century. The armoury is one of the world's best and reflects Stibbert's sideline as a scholar of military history. It includes some priceless pieces of European, Middle Eastern and Japanese weaponry. The Stibbert family apartments showcase a collection of tapestries, applied arts, paintings and costumes. One of the most important items is the 'Italian uniform' of Napoleon I.

Fortezza da Basso

2 Fortezza da Basso
B

Museo Stibbert

1
C

Via Frederico Stibbert
☎ 055 475-520
⊙ Summer: Fri-Wed: 10am-1pm & 3pm-6pm. Thu: closed.
Winter: Fri-Wed: 10am-2pm. Sat-Sun: 10am-6pm. Thu: closed.
Compulsory guided tours on the hour every day.
Admission charge.
2 admissions for the price of one with voucher on page 69.
also
Musei Fiorentini discount-2 carnets for the price of 1 (carnet comprises 10 coupons for 50% discount on admission to participating museums and galleries) with voucher on page 71.

The Arno and Southern Florence

There has been a bridge at the narrowest point of the River Arno since Roman times. Today's so-called 'Old Bridge', **Ponte Vecchio**, dates from 1345. Its three arches, resting on two massive boat-shaped piers, were designed to withstand the regular flooding of the river. The bridge replaced a late 10th-century structure that had been washed away when the river broke its banks in 1343.

The shops lining the original bridge would have contained butchers, blacksmiths, printmakers and tanners. They were generally badly built and constantly caught fire. When the bridge was rebuilt the shops were also built of stone.

In 1593 Grand Duke Ferdinando I, one of the last ruling Medicis, decided he could no longer bear the pollution caused by the bridge's 'vile' traders, and evicted the shop owners in favour of 50 goldsmiths and jewellers. The now-pedestrianised bridge still houses jewellers old and new, and in the middle of the bridge stands a bust of Benvenato Cellini, Florence's most famous goldsmith.

Some of the oldest shops on the Ponte Vecchio date from the late 14th century and have overhanging extensions propped up by sturdy wooden brackets, called *sporti*.

Ponte Vecchio

Ponte Vecchio

Exploring Florence: The Arno and Southern Florence · 41

On the bridge's south side is the defensive Mannelli Tower, part of the fortified house of the once-great Mannelli family. Also on the south approach to the bridge is a fountain made from a Roman sarcophagus, and a statue of *Bacchus* by Giambologna.

Fortunately, the Ponte Vecchio escaped danger during the Second World War, although it was the city's only bridge to do so. Today it is always a lively, popular place, with buskers and portrait painters competing with the jewellery shops that sell both modern and antique pieces. Overlooking the goings-on from the middle of the bridge, is a bust of the famous 16th-century Florentine goldsmith Benvenuto Cellini, which was positioned in 1900.

To celebrate Francesco de' Medici's marriage in 1565, Vasari was commissioned to construct a private corridor to allow the newly weds to move around the capital without mixing with ordinary people. The **Corridoio Vasariano** passes from the Palazzo Vecchio, through the Uffizi, across the east side of the Ponte Vecchio then in front of the church, Santa Felicìta, to the Palazzo Pitti.

Today the corridor contains some 700 paintings from the Medici's impressive private collection.

You enter the corridor in the Uffizi between halls 34 and 35. The section over the Ponte Vecchio has a selection of self-portraits – including Vasari, Bernini, Caracci, Rembrandt, Rubens, Velzqáuez, Dürer and Delacroix.

One of the oldest churches in Florence after San Lorenzo, **Santa Felicìta**, was founded in the 4th century by Greek settlers. It was remodelled in both the 11th and the 14th century – when it became a Medici family chapel – and then again in the 1730s by Ferdinando Ruggieri.

The church has retained many original Gothic and Renaissance features, most notably in the Cappella Capponi, the family chapel designed by Brunelleschi in 1420s. The chapel's claim to fame,

Corridoio Vasariano

Loggiato degli Uffizi 6
☎ 055 294-883
🕐 Closed temporarily from Nov 1998.

Santa Felicìta

Piazza di Santa Felicìta
☎ 055 213-018
🕐 Mon-Sat: 9am–12noon & 3.30pm-6pm
Sun: 9am-10am & 4.30pm-6pm.
Admission charge.

Exploring Florence: The Arno and Southern Florence

Palazzo Pitti

Piazza Pitti, Via Romana
🕒 Separate opening times for individual museums.

Palatine Gallery

Palazzo Pitti
☎ 055 238-8614
🕒 Tue-Sat: 8.30am-7pm. Sun: 8.30am-2pm. Mon: closed.

however, are the frescoes by Jacopo da Pontormo from the 1520s – the *Annunciation* and a highly erotic *Deposition*, whose bright colours are still startling.

Under the church's main cupola are portrayals of the four Evangelists, including *St. Mark* by Pontormo's pupil Agnolo Bronzino. In the right transept, the sacristy features a series by Taddeo Gaddi from around 1355.

Florence's largest and most opulent palace, **Palazzo Pitti**, was started in 1457 for a local banker, Luca Pitti, to rival the Medicis' more central palace. Following a design by Brunelleschi, the costs of construction finally ruined the Pitti family, who were forced to sell to their rivals in 1549.

The palace became the Medicis' main residence in 1550. They employed Ammannati to enlarge it and decorate it in their uniquely arrogant style – laying out the 45,000 square metres (484,200 square feet) of gardens at the rear. Over the next three centuries, the palace was continually expanded, with each addition respecting the overall design.

The Palazzo Pitti now contains a series of museums. Comparable to the Uffizi is the prestigious art collection at the **Palatine Gallery** on the palace's first floor. It was founded in the late 1700s to accommodate works from the Medici collection that would not fit in the Uffizi.

Today, the 26 rooms are strongest in 16th-century Italian art – especially Titian and Raphael – as well as boasting an enviable selection by Caravaggio, Rubens and Van Dyck. The rooms are hung three or four paintings deep in places – as they would have been originally – and ceilings have frescoes by Pietro da Cortona from the 1640s.

Among the better-known works on show are Raphael's *La Gravida* and *Madonna del Granduca*, Veronese's *Portrait of a Man*, Titian's *Portrait of an Englishman* and Filippo Lippi's *Virgin and Christ Child*.

The former summer apartments of the

Exploring Florence: The Arno and Southern Florence · 43

View of Florence from the south at dusk

Palazzo Pitti now contain the **Museo degli Argenti** (Silver Museum), a dazzling display of the ruling family's vast wealth – including an eye-boggling array of Florentine gold and silver work, Roman glassware, Chinese porcelain and German vases of turned ivory, all in lavishly frescoed rooms lined with portraits of the Medici.

Highlights of the collection include Lorenzo the Magnificent's own collection of antique vases, a compass made by Peter the Great and given to Cosimo III, and personal possessions of Caterina de' Medici.

The small **Museo delle Carrozze** (Carriage Museum) displays various stately carriages and sedan chairs from the 18th and 19th century courts of Lorraine and Savoy. *(Palazzo Pitti, ☎ 055 238-8614. ⏱ Tue-Sun: 8.30am-6.40pm.)*

On the third floor are 40 more rooms devoted to Italian, predominantly Tuscan, art from the period 1784 to 1924. Much of this collection was amassed by the Dukes of Lorraine and the rest was donated by the state. The undoubted highlight of this **Galleria d'Arte Moderna** (Modern Art Gallery) is a selection from the Macchiaio movement, the Italian version of Impressionism, including works by well-known locals Giovanni Boldini and Giovanni Fattori, along with Pucinelli, Zandomeneghi and Signorini.

Museo degli Argenti

Palazzo Pitti
☎ 055 238-8710
⏱ Tue-Sat: 8.30am-1.50pm. Open alternate Mondays and Sundays. Admission charge.

44 · Exploring Florence: The Arno and Southern Florence

There is also sculpture by Antonio Ciseri, furniture of the period, and two landscapes by Camille Pissaro. *(Palazzo Pitti, ☎ 055 238 86 16. ⏰ Tue-Sun: 8.30am-6.40pm.)*

Galleria del Costume

Palazzo Pitti
☎ 055 238 87 13
⏰ Tue-Sat: 8.30am-10pm. Sun: 8.30am-8pm.
Admission charge.

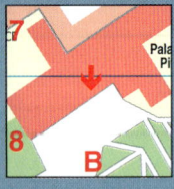

The south wing of the palace contains Italy's only fashion museum, the **Galleria del Costume** (Costume Gallery), which chronicles the changing fads of one of the world's most important fashion capitals from the late 1700s up to the 1980s.

Drawn from a collection of some 12,500 outfits and 1,000 accessories, the exhibition features items from the court of the Grand Dukes of Tuscany, including the richly embroidered dress that Eleanor de Toledo was buried in – immortalised in Bronzino's famous portrait in the Palazzo Vecchio. Newer exhibits include the trousseau of Lady Frana Florio, an early 20th-century debutante, flappers' fashions from the Roaring Twenties, and a 1980s Pucci dress.

Built in the south wing in the early 1600s,

Palazzo Pitti

the **Appartamenti Monumentali** (State Apartments) were revamped by the Dukes of Lorraine in the late 18th century and again in the last century when Florence was the capital of the Republic. The lavish Neo-Classical interiors are notable for their extravagant gold and stucco decoration, intended to impress visiting dignitaries.

The **Giardino di Bóboli** (Boboli Gardens)

Exploring Florence: The Arno and Southern Florence · 45

are one of the most impressive Italianate gardens in the world. They were laid out for Cosimo de Medici when he bought the nearby palace from the Pitti family in 1549. Work continued for over a hundred years to create the stunning arrangement with statues and fountains.

Close to the palace are formal gardens of clipped box hedges and an amphitheatre for the open-air performances of operas that the Medici enjoyed. The most famous feature in the gardens is the Grotta Grande by Buontalenti. Amid the imitation stalactites stand Giambologna's *Venus Bathing* and replicas of Michelangelo's *Slaves*, the originals of which once stood here.

The Isolotto, a spectacular island with a fountain by Giambologna, is reached by the Viottolone, an avenue of cypress trees lined with Roman statues. Near the main entrance, the well-known Bacchus Fountain by Cioli features Cosimo I's obese court dwarf, seated atop a turtle.

Various buildings are scattered throughout the gardens, including an orangery to nurture rare plants, a porcelain museum and the beautiful Kaffeehaus, built in 1776, which has magnificent views over the city.

The **Museo Zoologico 'La Specola'** (Zoological Museum) is part of the University of Florence's Natural History Museum and dates back to 1775. It was founded by the Grand Duke Pietro Leopoldo, and is the oldest scientific museum in Europe. It is known as "La Specola" after the astronomical tower or *specola* that topped the building until the late 1800s.

Ten of the 34 rooms are home to a huge collection of anatomical waxworks, many of which were manufactured in the 18th century as teaching tools, and display an admirable precision of detail. They demonstrate both human and animal anatomy.

Some of the earliest waxworks are the efforts of the famous Sicilian modeller Gaetano Zumbo, who worked for the Grand Duke Cosimo III until 1694. Other

---

Appartamenti Monumentali

Palazzo Pitti
☎ 055 238-8614
🕐 Tue-Sun: 8.30am-6.40pm. Mon: closed.
Admission charge.

Giardino di Bóboli

Piazza Pitti
☎ 055 212-688
🕐 Mon-Sun: Dec-Feb: 9am-4.30pm. Mar & Oct: 9am-5.30pm. Apr, May & Sep: 9am-6.30pm. Jun-Aug: 9am-7.30pm.
Closed 1st and 4th Mon.
Admission charge.

Museo Zoologico "La Specola"

Via Romana 17
☎ 055 22 88 251
🕐 Thu-Tue: 9am-1pm.
Wed: closed.
Admission charge.
2 admissions for the price of 1 with voucher on page 69.

46 · Exploring Florence: The Arno and Southern Florence

Forte di Belvedere

Boboli Gardens
🕐 Mon-Sun: Dec-Feb: 9am-4.30pm. Mar & Oct: 9am-5.30pm. Apr, May & Sep: 9am-6.30pm. Jun-Aug: 9am-7.30pm. Closed 1st and 4th Mon. Admission charge.

Museo Bardini

Piazza de' Mozzi
☎ 055 234-2427
🕐 Mon-Tue & Thu-Sat: 9am-1.30pm. Sun: 8am-12.30pm. Wed: closed Admission charge.
Musei Fiorentini discount-2 carnets for the price of 1 (carnet comprises 10 coupons for 50% discount on admission to participating museums and galleries) with voucher on page 71.

highlights of this section are the macabre 'plague waxes' demonstrating the effects of syphilis and decomposition.

The other 24 rooms are devoted to zoology, and the exhibits cover many species of existing animals as well as some extinct ones. The displays, which comprise one of the largest collections of taxidermy in the world, incorporate dioramas showing the natural habitat of exotic animals, and recorded bird song in the Bird Galleries.

As part of the city's defences, the star-shaped **Forte di Belvedere** fortress was designed by Bernardo Buontalenti in 1590 for Grand Duke Ferdinando I, who was keen to protect the city from external threats and internal unrest.

From the eastern side of the fortress you can climb to the ramparts. From here you can see the centre of the fort which contains Ammannati's Palazzini di Belvedere of the 1560s, a favourite refuge of the Medicis.

The bastion's ramparts give magnificent views over Florence and the surrounding hills, while to the east lies the best-preserved section of the city walls, running to the Piazza G. Poggi. The fort features regular exhibitions in its vast interior.

The huge collection at the **Museo Bardini** was amassed by art dealer and antiquarian Stefano Bardini and was bequeathed to the city on his death in 1923, along with the palace he built in 1883. Using the remains of Renaissance churches and *palazzi* demolished when the Piazza della Repubblica was being constructed, he created a neo-Renaissance structure to provide the perfect showcase for his collection.

His taste was eclectic and personal, and items on display range from Persian carpets and Turkish ceramics to paintings, armour, chimney pieces, carved ceilings, sculptures and musical instruments from ancient times to the Baroque period.

Among the highlights of the museum are a headless statue by Pisano of the *Virgin Mary*, *St. John the Baptist* by Giambono,

Exploring Florence: The Arno and Southern Florence · 47

and a gilt *Virgin Mary and Christ figure* by Donatello.

Florence's main river crossing, **Ponte San Trìnita**, was built in 1567 by Ammannati to celebrate Cosimo II's war successes. This replaced an earlier wooden bridge of 1252 swept away in floods. Reams have been written about its graceful curving arches – so daring that it was thought too delicate to support traffic – and the supposed original design by Michelangelo.

The statues of the Four Seasons from the garden of Alessandro Accaiuoli were added in 1608 to celebrate Cosimo II's marriage to Maria of Austria – Spring and Summer lie at the north side, Autumn and Winter to the south.

Ponte San Trinita

The bridge was destroyed by the retreating German forces in 1944 and rebuilt stone by stone a decade later – using original construction techniques – after the demolished masonry had been dredged from the River Arno.

Running from the Ponte San Trinita to the Piazza San Felice is the aristocratic **Via Maggio**, which came into its own after the Medici took up residence in the nearby Pitti Palace in the 1550s. It is lined with magnificent 16th-century palazzi.

Most notable are the Palazzo Ricasoli-Firidolfi (no. 7) with its fine courtyard,

Giardino di Bóboli

48 · Exploring Florence: The Arno and Southern Florence

Santo Spirito

Piazza di Santa Spirito
☎ 055 210-030
🕓 Thu-Tue: 8.30am-12noon & 3.30pm-5.30pm. Wed: 8am-12noon.

Cenacolo di Santo Spirito

Piazza di Santa Spirito 29
☎ 055 287-043
🕓 Tue-Sun: 9am-1.30pm. Mon: closed. Admission charge.
Musei Fiorentini discount-2 carnets for the price of 1 (carnet comprises 10 coupons for 50% discount on admission to participating museums and galleries) with voucher on page 71.

San Frediano in Cestello

Piazza di Cestello
☎ 055 215-816
🕓 Mon-Sun: 9am-11.45am & 4.30pm-5.30pm.

and the ornate *sgraffito* facade of Palazzo di Bianca Cappello (no. 24-26), built by Buontalenti in the 1570s for Francesco I's mistress. The poets Robert Browning and Elizabeth Barrett Browning lived in the Casa Guidi on Piazza di San Felice from 1846–61.

Santo Spirito was one of Brunelleschi's last projects and possibly his most perfect composition. Begun in 1435, only the foundations and north end of the choir were finished when the architect died in 1446, but work continued until 1487. What Vasari described as the most beautiful church in the world was never finished. As a result of arguments about Brunelleschi's original designs, the facade was merely plastered over, forming a blank, featureless wall.

Inside the proportions are perfect. Huge colonnades dominate the clean lines of the nave, leading to an elaborate Baroque high altar by Caccini, dating from the early 17th century. Around the church radiate 38 side altars with some fine 15th- and 16th-century Renaissance artwork, including Filippino Lippi's *Nerli Altarpiece* of the 1480s in the south transept, and a marble sarcophagus by Rossellino.

Off the north side of the nave, the octagonal sacristy designed in the 1490s by Sangallo has an elaborate dome and lantern. It is reached by a vestibule which contains a fine vault by Cronaca.

The former refectory, **Cenacolo di Santo Spirito**, is to the left of the church entrance. It is the last remaining part of the Augustinian monastery complex that once adjoined San Spirito. One entire wall of the big room, which now contains a small but important collection of sculptures donated to Florence in 1946, is covered with an extraordinary fresco of *The Crucifixion* by Orcagna, commissioned by the Cambi di Napoleone family in the 1360s.

The Fondazione Romano, a collection of pieces ranging from pre-Romanesque sculpture to 15th-century works, includes carved bas-reliefs and architectural remains. Two stone panels from the

Exploring Florence: The Arno and Southern Florence · 49

Basilica of Sant' Antonio in Padua date from around 1450 and are attributed to Donatello. There are several figures from the 1320s by Tino di Camaino, including *Caryatid* and the *Adoring Angel*. A particularly significant work is the *Virgin and Child* by Jacopo della Quercia.

Dominated by the plain plastered facade of the church, the **Piazza di Santo Spirito** is planted as a garden at the hub of the furniture restorers' quarter.

Cenacolo di Santo Spirito

The undoubted highlight of the square is the Palazzo Guadagni at no. 10, built in 1505 by Cronaca, with the city's first open loggia high up on the fourth floor. It is lined with many family-run trattorias, which serve good, inexpensive food. There is also a lively market held here daily.

Overlooking the River Arno, the bare stone exterior of the **San Frediano in Cestello** church is a local landmark in the wool and leather industry areas. Rebuilt in 1680 by Antonio Maria Ferri, the Latin cross has three side chapels decorated with stucco and paintings.

Especially notable are a 14th-century wooden *Madonna and Child* by a follower of Pisano, and a fine *Crucifixion* in the sacristy by 15th-century artist Jacopo del Sellaio.

The church of Santa Maria del Carmine burnt down in the 1770s and was rebuilt in the Baroque style. Luckily the small **Cappella Brancacci** (Brancacci Chapel) escaped the blaze, complete with the cycle of masterful 15th-century frescoes by court painter Masolino and his pupil Masaccio.

Cappella Brancacci

Piazza del Carmine
☎ 055 238-2195
⏲ Mon & Wed-Sat: 10am-4.30pm. Sun: 1pm-4.30pm. Tue: closed.
Admission charge.
Musei Fiorentini discount-2 carnets for the price of 1 (carnet comprises 10 coupons for 50% discount on admission to participating museums and galleries) with voucher on page 71.

50 · Exploring Florence: The Arno and Southern Florence

Piazzale Michelangelo

Porta San Niccolò

San Salvatore al Monte

Viale Galileo Galilei
Mon-Sun: 8am–
12noon & 2pm-5pm.

The two artists decorated the chapel for four years in the 1420s before Masaccio went to work in Rome, where he died at the age of just 25. Sixty years later the great Filippino Lippi finished the frescoes.

Masolino worked on the right side of the chapel, and Masaccio on the left, allowing their styles to be vividly contrasted. Where the master painted in the elegant International Gothic style, his pupil was more forceful, emotional and realistic – heralding the style of the new Renaissance age with his freedom of expression. Compare Masolino's elegant *Temptation of Adam and Eve* with the raw shame in Masaccio's *Expulsion of Adam and Eve from the Garden of Eden*.

Best known of the frescoes is Masaccio's *Payment of the Tribute*, which skilfully tells a story of three parts in a single frame. Such was the reputation of the frescoes that both Michelangelo and Leonardo da Vinci came here to study them.

Filippino Lippi's contribution to the chapel is most notable on the right-hand wall in the enormously powerful *Release of St. Peter*.

The **Piazzale Michelangelo**, the 'Balcony of Florence', was laid out on a slope close to the River Arno between 1865 and 1870. It was designed by Giuseppe Poggi to give an impressive panoramic view over the terracotta rooftops of the city. Copies of some of Michelangelo's most famous works dot the square, including a bronze David and statues from the Medici tombs in San Lorenzo. Unfortunately, it is usually filled with parked cars and souvenir stalls.

Next to the river on Piazza G. Poggi, the **Porta San Niccolò** is one of the original gates in the 14th-century city walls, and is the only one to retain its height. On the north side of the gate is a lunette of the *Virgin and Child* by an unknown artist.

The finest stretch of the city wall runs from here to the Fortezza di Belvedere via the Porta San Miniato.

The simple **San Salvatore al Monte** church, built between 1499 and 1504 by

Exploring Florence: The Arno and Southern Florence · 51

Cronaca, has just a single nave with side chapels.

The side chapels almost all contain 17th- and 18th-century canvases, as well as some fine 16th-century stained glass. There is also a terracotta *Deposition* from the 1520s by Giovanni della Robbia, and a bust of Florentine statesman Marcello Adriani.

The Carolingian foundation of **San Miniato al Monte** dates from 1018, when the present beautiful church overlooking Florence was begun. Its exquisite white and green marble facade was completed between 1090 and 1270, and shows the transition between Romanesque and Renaissance styles.

Inside, the floor of inlaid marble dates from 1207 and depicts the signs of the zodiac. Ahead, the Cappella del Crocifisso has a 1448 tabernacle by Michelozzo, while the Cappella del Cardinale del Portogallo features a fine carved tomb and terracotta decorations by della Robbia.

The sacristy from the 1380s contains frescoed scenes from the life of St. Benedict by Spinello Aretino. St. Benedict is also the focus in the cloister, where the frescoes have been attributed to Paolo Uccello.

The crypt contains an earlier chapel from the 11th century, with the original altar housing the relics of San Minias.

San Miniato al Monte

Via Monte alle Croci
☎ 055 234-2731
⏱ Mon-Sun: 8am–12.30pm & 2pm–7pm.

View from Piazzale Michelangelo

Beyond the City

Some 8km (5 miles) northeast of Florence is the Etruscan settlement of **Fièsole**, founded in 7 BC. When Julius Caesar founded nearby Florence in the first century BC, it soon overtook Fièsole as the centre of the region and made the hilltop town a satellite suburb for aristocrats.

The town's hub is the **Piazza Mino**, bordered by the Gothic town hall or **Palazzo Pretorio**, the church of **Santa Maria Primerana** with its notable frescoes, and the 11th-century **Duomo**, which incorporated Roman capitals into its nave. Don't miss the two pieces inside by local artist Mino da Fièsole – the carved tomb of Bishop Saluati and the *Madonna and Saints* on the altar.

Fièsole's ancient past is on show in its **Archaeological Park**. This has a 3,000-seat Roman theatre, which is still used for performances, baths and a temple, as well as the older Etruscan town walls. The nearby **Museo Faesulanum** displays local finds from Roman, Etruscan and Bronze Age days in a mock Roman temple.

West of the main square is the ancient church of **Sant'Alessandro**. The church's Neo-Classical facade hides its Romanesque interior. Nearby is the friary of **San Francesco**, which was built in the 14th century on the site of an acropolis. Just over 1km (0.5 miles) outside town is **San Domenico**, where Fra' Angelico was once a monk and painted a *Madonna and Angels* for the church.

Located about 80km (50 miles) downstream on the River Arno, **Pisa** is easily accessed by bus, train or car from Florence. The city is most visited for its so-called Field of Miracles, a fabulous religious complex featuring the cathedral, baptistery, enclosed cemetery and the legendary **Leaning Tower** – all sinking into the perilously marshy soil at different rates.

The complex of gleaming white marble buildings was begun in 1063 when the Romanesque **Duomo** was started. A masterpiece of Pisan Gothic style, the

---

Did You Know ...?

The modern Italian language has, since the 15th century, been based on the Tuscan dialect.

Beyond the City · 53

facade incorporates Moorish elements in its design. The undoubted masterpiece of the cathedral is Giovanni Pisano's carved pulpit, whose panels seem to glow with life.

The circular **Baptistery** – Italy's largest – was begun in 1150 and the delicate tracery and sequence of statues on the facade belies a surprisingly plain inside. Nicola Pisano's groundbreaking pulpit, companion piece to his son's in the cathedral, stands at the centre of a vast empty space and set the style of pulpits for centuries to come.

The Leaning Tower of Pisa

The **Camposanto** is a medieval cemetery, built around four sides like a cloister. Outstanding frescoes that once covered the walls were destroyed by a bomb in 1944 and just a few fragments remain, including Gozzoli's fabulous Old Testament scenes, along with the *Triumph of Death* and *Last Judgement*.

The iconic **Leaning Tower** – the complex's belltower – has always leaned, beginning its sideways journey in the early 1200s and continuing to its current 5.4 metres (17 feet) off the vertical. Delicate Romanesque arches stack up over the eight storeys, crowned by a bell chamber, giving the tower a wedding cake appearance. The tower has been closed to the public for several years, and bells are no longer rung for fear of worsening the problem.

The rest of the town is hardly on the same monumental scale, but is worth a wander. The **Piazza dei Cavalieri** is surrounded by buildings mostly designed by Vasari,

54 · Beyond the City

including the famous university of the **Scuola Normale Superiore**. On the riverfront is the little Gothic gem of **Santa Maria della Spina**, built to house a thorn from the Crown of Thorns. It was from the belltower of the church of San Nicola that Galileo displayed his new telescope to Cosimo II.

An express bus journey 48km (30 miles) to the south leads to **Siena**. This beautiful town straddles seven hills, and boasts twisting and climbing cobbled streets. Its golden age lasted from the 1260s to the 1340s, when the Black Death wiped out much of its population. A quiet 650 years since that time means that its ancient buildings and works of art have been perfectly preserved.

The town radiates from **Piazza del Campo**, a fan-shaped square bordered by *palazzi* whose ground floors have been converted into cafés. On the south side of the piazza is the vast Gothic **Palazzo Publico**, which still serves as the town hall after 650 years. Inside are some vivid frescoes and the **Museo Civico**, whose works of art include Lorenzetti's famous *Maestà*. The building's **Torre del Mangia** belltower gives stunning views over the town and countryside, right down to the exquisitely carved marble basin of the **Fonte Gaia**.

Siena's **Duomo** dates from the 1130s, encompassing both the Romanesque and Gothic periods in one of Italy's most memorable cathedrals. The distinctive black and white marble striped facade incorporates Moorish mosaics.

Legend has it that wishes made when touching the brass doors will come true. The **Piccolomini Library**, too, harbours Pinturicchio's masterly frescoes of the life of Pope Pius II from the early 1500s.

Three religious foundations from the 1200s dominate Siena's skyline. They are the houses of the Domenican, Franciscan and Servite orders, which all still contain art treasures. The **Pinacoteca Nazionale** is Siena's art gallery, with some fine religious paintings of the 13th and 14th centuries, including several works by the Lorenzetti brothers.

Reflections

'The traveller who has gone to Italy to study the tactile values of Giotto, or the corruption of the Papacy, may return remembering nothing but the blue sky and the men and women who live under it' – E.M. Forster, *A Room with a View*

Beyond the City · 55

The picture-postcard countryside south of is Italy's most famous wine-producing area, yielding the fine Chianti reds. There are plenty of tasting opportunities for the visitor in the local villages that are dotted around the region – for example **Greve**, **Panzano**, **Gaiole**.

North of Florence are the attractive old towns of **Pistoia** and **Prato**, which make interesting day trips. In the walled town of **Lucca**, a Roman street plan is still apparent – especially in the main square with its clear amphitheatre shape.

South of Florence are two fascinating medieval towns. The famous towers of **San Gimignano** were built by rival families as protection and one-upmanship, and provide a stunning skyline even though only 14 of the original 76 still stand.

Close by is **Volterra**, a pleasant little medieval town at the heart of an alabaster-producing region. Volterra's Etruscan past is well documented in the most important museum of the period in Italy. If the Medici fascinate you, there are several villas around Florence. The palatial **Villa di Poggio a Caiano** gives a clue to the level of luxury the ruling family demanded. More modest is the **Villa di Castello**, the garden of which still boasts sculpture, mazes and fountains. The **Villa della Petraia** was a castle made into a palace, while the **Villa dell'Artimino** was a glorified hunting lodge.

Piazza del Campo, Siena

Dining

Piazza della Signorina

Hemingway
Café

Piazza Piattellina 9
Tue-Thu: 4.30pm-1am. Fri & Sat: 4.30pm-2am. Sun & Mon: closed.

Food is a taken seriously in Tuscany, and deservedly so. The delicious specialities for which Tuscany is so well-known have remained more or less unchanged since the Renaissance. The staple ingredients include tomatoes, beans, sheep's milk cheeses, hams and salamis. Simple grilled or roast meats, generously seasoned with herbs and high-quality olive oil, and dried salt cod are some of the rustic peasant dishes found on many menus.

Lunch *(pranzo)* is traditionally eaten at 1pm and supper *(cena)* at about 9pm. Since it is more expensive eating at a table, it is worth considering having a quicker snack standing at the counter.

Bars will often sell a selection of filled rolls *(panini)* and sandwiches *(tramezzini)*. For spit-roast chicken head to a *rosticceria* and for take-away slices of pizza try one of the numerous *pizza taglia* scattered throughout the city.

Tasty and filling pastas and pizzas are found in *spaghettarias* and *pizzerias*, while slightly more extensive menus, and steeper prices, are on offer in *trattorias* and *ristorantes*.

Unlike many regions in Italy, where pasta often forms the bulk of a meal, Tuscan dishes are invariably eaten with chunks of the region's delicious traditional bread, which is baked without salt.

Dining · 57

Although there are almost no exclusively vegetarian eating establishments, there is still plenty of meat-free choice. Authentic Tuscan dishes include *ribollita* (a thick vegetable soup), *panzanella* (a salad of tomatoes, herbs and bread soaked in oil), and *fagioli all'uccelletto* (beans in a rich tomato sauce).

Even more so than in the rest of Italy, the ice-cream in Florence is delicious. Alternative desserts include *panforte*, a heavily spiced and very dense cake with whole almonds, and *cantucci*, sweet hard biscuits eaten dipped in *vin santo*, a dessert wine.

Tuscany's local Chianti wines make a perfect accompaniment to any meal, and the reds from the Classico and Rufina areas are particularly good. A refreshing alternative is Italian beer, notably Peroni or Moretti.

Adding both a cover charge and a 10 per cent service charge to the bill *(il conto)* is virtually standard. Where service is not included, a 12–15 per cent tip is expected.

Cafés and bars

Caffè Gilli *(Piazza della Repubblica 36. ⏰ Wed-Mon: 8am-midnight.)*

Caffè Italiano *(Via della Condotta 56. ⏰ Mon-Sat: 8am-8pm & 9.30pm-1am.)*

Caffèlatte *(Via degli Alfani 39. ⏰ Mon-Sat: 8am-1am.)*

Gelaterias and pasticcerias

Ruggini *(Via de' Neri 76. ⏰ Tue-Sat: 7.30am-8pm. Sun: 7am-1.30pm.)*

Vivoli *(Via Isole delle Stinche 7. ⏰ Tue-Sun: 8am-1am.)*

Restaurants

Alle Murate. *(Via Ghibellina 52. ⏰ Tue-Sun: 7pm-12midnight. Mon: closed.)*

Antellesi *(Via Faenza 9. ⏰ Mon-Fri: 12.30-2.30pm & 7.30-11.30pm.)*

La Libra *(Via Carducci 5. ⏰ Mon-Fri: 12.30-2pm & 8pm-12midnight.)*

Tramvai *(Piazza T. Tasso 14. ⏰ Mon-Fri: 12noon-3pm & 7-10pm.)*

Festival del Gelato
Ice Cream

Via del Corso 75
⏰ Tue-Sat: 8am-8pm
Sun: 7am-2pm. Mon: closed.

Danny Rock
Café-Restaurant

Via Pandolfini 13
⏰ Mon-Sun: 3pm-1am.

Za Za
Trattoria

Piazza del Mercato Centrale 26
⏰ Mon-Sat: 12noon-3pm & 7-11pm. Sun: closed.

Shopping

Florence's shops are generally open between Monday and Saturday from around 9am, closing at 1pm, then reopening from 4pm to 7 or 8pm. They often close on Saturday afternoons during summer, on Monday mornings in winter and for the whole of August.

Florence is not a high-fashion city, but shopping here can be blissful. High-class designer fashion is found on **Via Tornabuoni**, such as **Versace** *(nos. 13–15)*, **Ferragamo** *(no. 16)*, **Gucci** *(no. 73)*, and department store **Beltrami** *(no. 48)*. **Via della Vigna Nova** offers similarly priced labels, with **Giorgio Armani** *(no. 51)*, **Emilio Pucci** *(no. 97)* and **Valentino** *(no. 47)*.

Less expensive outlets are along the popular pedestrianised **Via de' Calzaiuoli**, especially department store **Coin** *(no. 56)*. Other pedestrianised roads around **Piazza della Repubblica** are equally good value, especially **Via del Corso** and **Via Roma**.

Florence's street markets are usually very lively. The city's central market, and the one most visited by tourists, is **Mercato di San Lorenzo**, which has hundreds of stalls selling clothes and leather goods. It's not the place for bargain hunting and you should be prepared to haggle with stallholders, but the atmosphere is fun. The market is open from 9am til 7.30pm throughout the week, except for Sunday.

Nearby is the cast-iron and glass covered **Mercato Centrale**, the city's main food market. Its stalls are laden with fresh produce, including prepared fish, meats, cheeses and fruit perfect for a picnic lunch.

Right in the city centre is the **Mercato Nuovo**, or Straw Market. Here you will find leather goods and souvenirs every day apart from Sunday. The **Mercato delle Pulci**, or Flea Market, is a general bric-à-brac and antiques market held every Sunday. It is particularly large and vibrant on the last Sunday of every month.

Florence is famous for its leather goods, particularly its small leather-covered boxes, which abound in both the street markets

---

Versace

13–15 Via Tornabuoni

Mercato Centrale
Food

Piazza del Mercato Centrale
Mon–Fri: 7am–2pm.

I Sapori del Chianti
Food and Drink

Via de' Servi 10

Shopping · 59

and shops. **Beltrami** *(Via de' Tornabuoni 48)* is a leather department store with bags, shoes, clothes and belts, **La Pelle** *(Via Guicciardini 11)* has young and trendy clothes, **Madova** *(Via Guicciardini 2)* sells every kind of leather glove on the market, while **Eusebio** *(Via del Corso 5)* has inexpensive men's and women's shoes.

Also popular is the locally made hand-marbled paper used to cover books, pencils, picture frames and so on. There is a good selection at **Giannini** *(Piazza Pitti 37)* and **Il Torchio** *(Via dei Bardi 17)*.

Tuscan food and wine can be well worth stocking up on while in Florence. **I Sapori del Chianti** sells nothing but the local produce of Chianti, including wine, olive oil, salami and condiments. **Pegna** *(Via della Studio 26)* is a good general supermarket with a wide variety of local foodstuffs at normal retail prices, and **Enoteca Bonatti** *(Via Vincenzo Gioberti 66-68)*, off Piazza Cesare Baccaria, has fine wines and olive oils from just outside Florence.

Florence still has links with its gold-working past. Jewellery has been made by **Torrini** *(Piazza del Duomo 10)* for 600 years, while **Il Gatto Bianco** offers a more contemporary angle on silver and gold. The shops that line the **Ponte Vecchio** almost all sell jewellery but cater solely to the tourist trade – with prices to match.

Pegna

Via della Studio 26

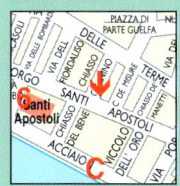

Il Gatto Bianco

Borgo Santi Apostoli 12

A souvenir stall

Nightlife

For a city whose tourist appeal lies predominantly in its architectural and artistic heritage, it can come as something of a surprise that Florence's nightlife is quite so buzzing.

The tourist office on Via Cavour has details of the many evening events in town, or you could buy a copy of the city's weekly listings guides *Metró* or *Time Off*.

Few restaurants serve food after midnight, but you can pick up a bite from the renowned **Bar Mercato Ortofrutticolo** every day until 3am. Funky **Capocaccia** *(Lungarno Corsini 120)* where you can eat – at a price – until after 1am, is another option. San Niccolò's **La Torre**, *(Lungarno Cellini 65)* is more low-key and stays open until 5am.

The **Art Bar** *(Via del Moro 4)* is all cocktails and sophistication, in competition for the designer-clad beautiful people with **Papillon** *(Piazza del Duomo 1)*. The more budget-minded should head for the **Gap Café** *(Via dei Pucci 5)* with low-price drinks, or the more stylish **Rex Café** *(Via Fiesolana 25)* which stays open until 2am. If you have a hankering for an Irish pub, try the **Old Stove**.

Florence's nightclub scene doesn't get started until at least 11pm as Italians tend to eat late and make mealtimes very social occasions. Even though Florence is a conservative city, the young university population makes sure there is plenty of life after dark.

The best disco in town – and also its most popular – is **Meccanò**, always packed to bursting point and filled with the young and trendy. Even more modish is **Central Bar** *(Parco delle Cascine)* where the beautiful people dance to the latest in jungle and hip hop. **Space Electronic** *(Via Palazzuolo 37)* looks like a trip back to the 70s with its videos, glass dancefloor and lasers. The most sumptuous club is the **Lido** *(Lungarno Pecori Giraldi 1)* overlooking the River Arno.

The biggest venue for live music is **Palasport** *(Viale Paoli)*, where the biggest

---

Bar Mercato Ortofrutticolo
Bar and Restaurant

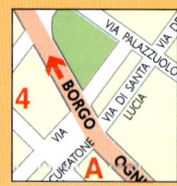

Viale Guidoni 46, Novoli

Cafe Rex
Bar

Via Fiesolana 25

Old Stove
Irish Pub

Via Pelliceria 24

Meccanò
Nightclub

Viale degli Olmi 1

Nightlife · 61

pop concerts take place, while **Tenax** *(Via Pratese 46)* draws a constant stream of international bands in a more intimate venue that transforms itself into a high-energy disco when the bands leave the stage.

Pegaso *(Via Palazzuolo 82)* is the city's leading jazz venue with music from 10pm to after 2am. The **Jazz Café** *(Via Nuova de Caccini 3)* is choosy about who it lets in, but has live sets every Friday and Saturday night. **Betty Boop** *(Via Altani 26)* has more varied acts that include rock, cabaret and jazz.

The two main classical venues are the **Teatro Comunale**, the home of a symphony orchestra, ballet company and opera company, and the **Teatro Verdi** *(Via Ghibellina 99, ☎ 055 239 6242)*, with its leading opera and ballet performances, musicals and pop concerts. The **Teatro della Pergola** *(Via della Pergola 12, ☎ 055 247 9651)* has a programme of Italian classics from October to May and chamber music and small operas the rest of the year, while the **Teatro Niccolini** has contemporary and innovative Italian drama from October to May. The bigger churches hold classical music concerts all year round.

The **Maggio Musicale Fiorentino** is one of Italy's leading festivals of opera and classical music, lasting from April to July. The orchestra, chorus and ballet company perform at **Teatro Verdi**, **Teatro della Pergola** and the **Teatro Comunale**.

Few cinemas offer films in their native language, choosing instead to dub foreign films into Italian. To see films in English, head to the **Cinema Astro** *(Piazza San Simone)*.

Teatro Comunale

Corso Italia 16
☎ 055 277-9236

Teatro Niccolini

Via Ricasoli 3
☎ 055 239-6653

The Duomo at night

Visitor Information

Detail from the Neptune Fountain

CHILDREN

Florence is a wonderful education for children with an interest in art, and as in the rest of Italy, youngsters are made very welcome in restaurants.

ELECTRIC CURRENT

Electricity in Italy runs on 220V, so British appliances simply need a two-prong convertor, which is available at airports. American 110V appliances need a transformer.

ETIQUETTE

When visiting churches, dress modestly and avoid shorts and bare shoulders. Good manners when greeting shopkeepers and other strangers is expected.

Italians only drink alcohol with meals, and any display of drunkenness is met with disapproval. Smoking is widespread and is banned only on public transport.

HEALTH AND SAFETY

Emergency hospital treatment is free for visitors from other EU countries. All visitors are advised to take out comprehensive travel insurance which includes medical coverage.

For emergency medical treatment, go to the casualty department of the Santa Maria Nuova hospital *(Piazza Santa Maria Nuova 1, ☎ 055 275 81)*.

CUSTOMS

Import restrictions for non-EU residents are:
Tobacco: 200 cigarettes or 100 cigars; **Alcohol**: 2 litres of wine plus 1 litres of spirits; **Perfumes**: 50g.

Visitor Information · 63

Pickpockets are quite common in Florence, so take care in busy or particularly touristy areas.

Whilst not as marked as in some other Italian cities, visiting women, especially blondes, may feel uncomfortable with the excess attentions of Italian men. As elsewhere, dressing soberly will mean you are noticed less.

HOTELS

Below is a selection of hotels for various budgets in the centre of Florence. 👛 = L60,000 for a standard double room per night.

Excelsior *(Piazza Ognissanti 3, ☎ 055 264-201.)* 👛 👛 👛 👛 👛

Monna Lisa *(Borgo Pinti 27, ☎ 055 247-9751.)* 👛 👛 👛 👛

Kraft *(Via Solferino 2, ☎ 055 284-273.)* 👛 👛 👛 👛

Brunelleschi *(Piazza Santa Elisabette 3, ☎ 055 290-311.)* 👛 👛 👛 👛

Astoria *(Via del Giglio 9, ☎ 055 239-8095.)* 👛 👛 👛 👛

Balestri *(Piazza Mentana, ☎ 055 214-743.)* 👛 👛 👛

Aprile *(Via della Scala 6, ☎ 055 216 237.)* 👛 👛 👛

Annalena *(Via Romana 34, ☎ 055 222-402.)* 👛 👛 👛

Liana *(Via Alfieri 18, ☎ 055 245-303.)* 👛 👛

Nuova Italia *(Via Faenza 26, ☎ 055 287-508.)* 👛 👛

Azzi *(Via Faenza 56, ☎ 055 213-806.)* 👛

Bandini *(Piazza Santo Spirito 9, ☎ 055 215-308.)* 👛

LANGUAGE

The English language is widespread in Florence, especially in the tourist trade and most hotels. It's useful to know a few words of Italian, and the language is both easy and enjoyable to pronounce.

Hello	*Buon giorno*
Goodbye	*Arrivederci*

EMERGENCIES

Dial ☎ 112 for the police, ☎ 115 for the fire service and ☎ 118 for an ambulance.

64 · Visitor Information

LOST PROPERTY

Contact the **Ufficio dei Oggetti Smarriti del Comune** *(Via Circondaria 19, ☎ 367-943)* for items which may have been handed in to the police.

Excuse me, sorry	*Scusa*
Please	*Per favore*
Thank you	*Grazie*
How are you?	*Come sta?*
Do you speak English?	*Parla inglese?*
I don't understand	*Non capisco*
Where is...?	*Dov' è...*
Entrance	*Entrata*
Exit	*Uscita*
Open	*Aperto*
Closed	*Chiuso*
Help!	*Aiuto!*

MAIL / POST

The **Palazzo della Posta** (main post office) is at Via Pellicceria 8 *(☎ 055 216 122)* and is open Monday to Friday from 8am-7pm and on Saturdays until noon. Poste restante (*Fermo Posta*) letters should be sent here. Ensure that you have your passport as proof of identity when collecting letters.

Stamps can be bought at tobacconists (look out for the black and white *T* sign) or post offices.

Fresh produce at a Florentine grocers

MONEY

Italian bank notes come in denominations of 1,000, 2,000, 5,000, 10,000, 50,000, 100,000 and 500,000 *lire* (L), and coins of L500, L200, L100 and L50.

Telephone tokens (*gettoni*), which are worth L200, are in general circulation in the same way as small change.

You can exchange money at banks, the railway station, exchange offices or at the main post office (page 64), and international credit and debit cards can be used in some bank machines.

Most large establishments in the centre of Florence accept travellers' cheques, although the exchange rate might be quite high. Major credit cards are also widely accepted.

OPENING HOURS

Banks - Standard opening hours are 8.30am to 1pm and 3pm to 4pm Monday to Friday.

Bars / Restaurants - Cafés, restaurants and bars tend to close at about 10pm. Most restaurants close for at least one day a week.

Museums / Galleries - This guide lists individual opening times under each museum's entry.

Shops - Business hours are generally 9am to 1pm and 3pm or 4pm to 7pm Monday to Saturday. The majority are closed on Sunday and some close on Monday mornings or Wednesdays.

SPECIAL TRAVELLERS

Disabled - Facilities for those with impaired mobility are quite poor in Florence. The tourist information office is the best source of advice and information about access.

Elderly - Concessions are available with proof of age. Where specified in this guide, **for less** discounts are available on top of the normal senior discount.

Students - Concessions are available at many attractions and museums when acceptable ID, such as an ISIC card, is produced. Where specified in this guide, **for less** discounts are available on top of the normal student discount.

Gay - **ARCI-gay** (☎ 055 239-8772) is Italy's gay rights organisation and is a good source of listings and information.

TELEPHONES

Public phones are orange and accept cards, coins or *gettoni* (telephone tokens). For more expensive calls, it is helpful to know that the telephone centre at Via

PACKING

Summer in Florence can be sweltering, so bring light clothes. Make sure, however, that you can cover bare legs and shoulders to sightsee in churches.

Winter temperatures rarely drop below freezing, but take an umbrella. Spring and autumn are the best times to visit.

Horse-drawn carriage

Main Tourist Office

Via Cavour 1
☎ 055 290-832
⏰ Mon-Sat: 8am–2.pm.

Cavour allows visitors to make a call and pay for it afterwards.

International calls are expensive compared to many other European countries, but are cheaper after 10pm.

TIPPING

When service is not included in restaurants, leave a 15% tip. Lavatory attendants, church custodians, bellboys and other attendants normally expect a small tip.

TOURIST INFORMATION

The main **APT** (Italian State Tourist Board) office is at Via Cavour (☎ *055 290-832*), with a branch at Via A. Manzoni (☎ *055 233-205*). Both are open Monday-Saturday from 8am-2pm.

TOURS

Large hotels can arrange for knowledgeable English-speaking guides to show you around the city, and the **Florentine Tour Guides Society** (*Viale Gramsci 9a, ☎ 055 247-8188*) provides a similar, independent service.

The tourist office can give you details of companies running scheduled tours around the city. **SITA** (*Viale Cadorna 105, ☎ 055 483-651*) and **Universalturismo** (*Via Cavour 180R, ☎ 055 503-91*) are two such organisations, and they also provide guided coach trips to nearby places such as Pisa.

Visitor Information · 67

TRANSPORT AROUND THE CITY

Bus - Florence is a historic city that is best tackled on foot, but the bus service makes an efficient and reasonably priced alternative for those weary of walking. Tickets, which should be bought from bars or tobaconnists before travelling, must be validated in the orange machine as you board.

Most routes centre around the train station, and a plan of the bus network can be acquired from ticket outlets.

Taxi - Taxis may be hailed in the street or booked (☎ 43 90, 42 42 or 47 98). There is a minimum fare, with a further supplement after 10pm.

USEFUL TELEPHONE NUMBERS

Airport Information: ☎ *050 500-707 (Galileo Galilei);* ☎ *055 373-498.*

European Operator: ☎ *176.*

International Operator: ☎ *170.*

Main post office: ☎ *055 216-122.*

Main tourist office: ☎ *055 290-832 / 3.*

Pharmacy rota system: ☎ *167 420-707 (freephone).*

Pise Tourist Information Office: ☎ *050 500-707.*

Police station: ☎ *497-71.*

Telephone information: ☎ *12.*

Traffic police: ☎ *577-777.*

Youth Hostel: ☎ *055 268-338.*

TRANSPORT FROM THE AIRPORT

The nearest major airport to Florence is **Galileo Galilei**, 50 miles (80km) away in Pisa. There is a train service calling first at Pisa and then, after an hour, at Florence. Trains leave hourly until 11.40pm.

Florence has its own very small airport, **Amerigo Vespucci**, which is 3 miles (5km) away and handles mostly domestic flights. A bus service connects it with central Florence with a journey time of about 10 minutes.

CREDITS

Text:
Graham Parker

Principal photography:
A.F. Kersting, Mecky Fögeling, Photobank.

Rolling Tuscan countryside

Index

Appartamenti
    Monumentali 44
Archaeological Park,
    Fièsole 52

Badia Fiorentina 25
Baptistery, Pisa 53
Battistero di San
    Giovanni 11

Campanile 12
Camposanto, Pisa 53
Cappella Brancacci 49,50
Casa Buonarroti 26
Casa di Dante 25
Cenacolo di
    Sant'Apollonia 39
Cenacolo di Santo Spirito 48
Chianti 55
Children 62
Commune di Firenze
    Museo Fiorentino 15
Conservatorio Musicale
    Luigi Cherubini 38
Corridoio Vasariano 41
Customs 62

Dining 56
Duomo, Fièsole 52
Duomo, Pisa 52
Duomo, Siena 54

Eboristeria 21
Electric Currency 62
Etiquette 62

Fièsole 52
Fonte Gaia, Siena 54
Forte di Belvedere 46
Fortezza da Basso 39

Galleria d'Arte Moderna 43
Galleria del Costume 44
Galleria dell'Accademia 38
Giardino dei Semplici 36
Giardino di Bóboli 44,45
Green Cloister 15

Husband's Chamber 30
Health and Safety 62
Hotels 63

Language 64
Leaning Tower, Pisa 52
Lost Property 64
Lucca 55

Mail / Post 64
Mercato Nuovo 19
Money 64
Museo Alinari 15
Museo Archeologico 34
Museo Bardini 46
Museo del Bigallo 12
Museo Civico, Siena 54

Museo degli Argenti 43
Museo della Carozze 43
Museo della Fondazione
    H.P.Horne 29
Museo dell'Opera di
    Santa Croce 28
Museo di Firenze com'era 33
Museo di Storia della
    Scienza 20
Museo Ebraico di Firenze 35
Museo e Chiostri
    Monumentali 15
Museo Faesulanum,
    Fièsole 52
Museo Fiorentino 15
Museo Marino Marini 16
Museo Nazionale del
    Bargello 26
Museo Nazionale di Antropologia
    ed Ethnologia 13
Museo Stibbert 39
Museo Zoologica
    'La Specola' 45

Nightlife 60

Ognissanti 16
Opening Hours 65
Opficio delle Pietre Dure 37
Orsanmichele 19

Packing 65
Palatine Gallery 42
Palazzo Corsini 17
Palazzo della Casa
    di Risparmio 22
Palazzo della Crocetta 34
Palazzo degli Uffizi 23
Palazzo Corsi-Alberti 29
Palazzo Nonfinito 13
Palazzo Pitti 42
Palazzo Pretorio, Fièsole 52
Palazzo Publico, Siena 54
Palazzo Pucci 32
Palazzo Rucellai 16
Palazzo Vecchio 22
Piazza del Campo, Siena 54
Piazza della Repubblica 35
Piazza dell Signoria 21
Piazza dei Cavalieri, Pisa 53
Piazza dei Ciompi 34
Piazza di San Lorenzo 32
Piazza di Santa Spirito 49
Piazzale Michelangelo 50
Piazza Mino, Fièsole 52
Piazza Santissima
    Annunziata 37
Piccolomini Library, Siena 54
Pinacoteca Nazionale,
    Siena 54
Pisa 52
Pistoia 55
Ponte Santi Trínita 47
Ponte Vecchio 40
Porta San Niccolò 50

Prato 55

Raccolta di Arte Contemporanea
    'Alberto della Ragione' 22
Reliquary of the Title
    of the Cross 15

San Domenico, Fièsole 52
San Francesco, Fièsole 52
San Frediano in
    Cestello 49
San Lorenzo 31
San Marco 35
San Miniato al Monte 51
San Pancrazio 16
San Salvatore al Monte 50,51
Santa Apostoli 18
Santa Croce 27
Santa Felicità 41
Sant' Alessandro,
    Fièsole 52
Santa Maria della
    Spina, Pisa 54
Santa Maria del Fiore
    (the Duomo) 10
Santa Maria Primarana,
    Fièsole 52
Santa Maria Maddalena
    dei Pazzi 34
Santa Maria Novella 14
Santa Trinita 17
Santissima Annunziata 37
Santo Spirito 48
Santo Stefano al Ponte 20
Scuola Normale
    Superiore, Pisa 54
Shopping 58
Siena 54
Spanish Chapel 15
Special Travellers 65
Spedale degli Innocenti 37

Telephones 65
Tempio Israelitico 35
Tipping 66
Torre del Mangia, Siena 54
Tourist Information 66
Tours 66
Transport around the
    city 67
Transport from the
    Airport 67

Useful Telephone
    Numbers 67

Vestments of St. Thomas 15
Via Maggio 47
Villa dell'Artiminio 55
Villa della Petraia 55
Villa di Castello 55
Villa di Poggio a Caiano 55
Volterra 55

Wife's Chamber 30

Vouchers · 69

Musei Fiorentini

This voucher entitles the holder to 2 **Comune di Firenze Musei Fiorentini** carnets for the price of 1. Carnets comprise ten tickets giving 50% off admission to the participating museums.

Valid from October 1, 1999

Casa Buonarroti

2 admissions for the price of 1 at the **Casa Buonarroti** (page 26)

Valid from October 1, 1999

Museo Stibbert

2 admissions for the price of 1 at the **Museo Stibbert** (page 39)

Valid from October 1, 1999

Museo Zoologico "La Specola"

2 admissions for the price of 1 at the **Museo Zoologica "La Specola"** (page 45)

Valid from October 1, 1999

70 · Vouchers

for less

Il possessore di questo tagliando ha il diritto al seguente sconto:

2 per 1: un Carnet gratuito per i **Musei Fiorentini del Comune di Firenze** con l'acquisto di ogni Carnet. Vedere informazioni dei Musei e Gallerie participanti.

for less

Il possessore di questo tagliando ha il diritto al seguente sconto nel **Casa Buonarroti** (p. 26):

2 ingressi al prezzo di 1: una entrata gratuita con una entrata del stesso o piu' costoso valore

for less

Il possessore di questo tagliando ha il diritto al seguente sconto nel **Museo Stibbert** (p. 39):

2 ingressi al prezzo di 1: una entrata gratuita con una entrata del stesso o piu' costoso valore

for less

Il possessore di questo tagliando ha il diritto al seguente sconto nel **Museo Zoologico "La Specola"** (p. 45):

2 ingressi al prezzo di 1: una entrata gratuita con una entrata del stesso o piu' costoso valore

Vouchers and Customer Response Card · 71

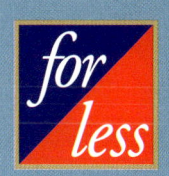

Museo della Fondazione H. P. Horne

for less

2 admissions for the price of 1 at the **Museo della Fondazione H. P. Horne** (page 30)

Valid from October 1, 1999

Customer Response Card

We would like to hear your comments about the *Florence for less Compact Guide* so that we can improve it. Please complete the information below and mail this card. One card will be picked out at random to win a free holiday.
No stamp is required, either in Italy or your own country.

Name: ....

Address: ....

Tel. no.: ....

If you bought the book, where did you buy it from?..

....

If you were given the book, which tour operator gave it to you? ....

Number of people travelling in your party? ....

How many days were you in Florence? ....

Did you like the guidebook?...

What did you like about it?...

....

Would you recommend it to a friend?..........................

Would you be more interested in a tour operator's package if you knew it included the *Florence for less Compact Guide*? ....

....

Any other comments..

....

....

72 · Vouchers and Customer Response Card

for less

Il possessore di questo tagliando ha il diritto al seguente sconto nel **Museo della Fondazione H. P. Horne** (p. 30):

2 ingressi al prezzo di 1: una entrata gratuita con una entrata del stesso o piu' costoso valore

NE PAS AFFRANCHIR
NO STAMP REQUIRED

REPONSE PAYEE
GRANDE-BRETAGNE

Metropolis International (UK) Limited
222 Kensal Road
LONDON, GREAT BRITAIN
W10 5BN

IBRS/CCRI NUMBER: PHQ-D/2560/W

By air mail
Par avion